A Guide to the Historic Houses, Churches and Other Points of Interest of Beaufort, South Carolina

A Guide to
Historic Beaufort

Revised Ninth Edition

Historic Beaufort
FOUNDATION

Acknowledgements

This Revised Ninth Edition of *A Guide to Historic Beaufort*
was made possible through financial assistance received from the
Beaufort County Accommodations Grant Program
and Main Street Beaufort, USA.

Substantial new information and photography for this edition was provided by the
Beaufort County Above Ground Historic Resource Survey (1998) compiled by Brockington
Associates Inc., in association with Brooker Architectural Design Consulting,
Historic Beaufort Foundation, and Preservation Consultants, Inc. The survey was funded
in part by Beaufort County, the City of Beaufort, the Town of Port Royal,
and Federal Funds from the National Park Service, U. S. Department of the Interior,
administered by the South Carolina Department of Archives and History.

Special thanks are extended to Colin and Jane Bruce Brooker, Maxine Lutz, Wyatt Pringle,
and Susan Tritschler for their valuable input into this publication. In addition, thanks are extended to
the many property owners who have contributed information through the successive editions.

This edition is dedicated to the memory of David Herzbrun,
who assisted greatly with its preparation.

David B. Schneider, Editor
Louise Coleman, Design
Colin Brooker, Principal Photography

Additional Photography for the Revised Ninth Edition
Eric Horan, cover
Nancy E. White

ISBN 0-9657891-0-1
Library of Congress Catalog Card Number: 97-71741

Printed by Kennickell Printing, Savannah, Georgia

Historic Beaufort

Table of Contents

Historic Preservation in Beaufort

A little more than fifty years ago, a group of farsighted local citizens recognized that the historic buildings and settings that define the character of Beaufort were worthy of preserving for future generations. Banding together as the "Committee to Save the Lafayette Building," the group was successful in saving the Verdier House, as the Lafayette Building is now known, at 801 Bay Street. In 1967, the leadership of the committee realized that there was a need for broader action to protect other important landmarks. Historic Beaufort Foundation was organized.

In its first thirty years, Historic Beaufort Foundation has accomplished a great deal. The first architectural inventory of the city was completed in 1968 and a year later the Beaufort Historic District was listed on the National Register of Historic Places. A Revolving Fund was established in 1971 and since that time has been used to purchase and restore several important buildings. In 1975, the historic district was designated a National Historic Landmark, one of one four districts in South Carolina to have received this important honor. The Verdier House was restored in 1976 and now serves as an interpretation center for the historic architecture of Beaufort.

Historic Beaufort Foundation continues to be Beaufort's principal historic preservation advocate. Our active involvement in maintaining the historic district has made a significant contribution to its becoming a major destination for tourists and an attractive place in which to live and work. If you are not a member of the Foundation, we encourage you to join us.

Introduction

Beaufort's National Historic Landmark District is one of the treasures of America's heritage. Long recognized for its fine architecture and its antebellum past, the city also played an important role during the Civil War and Reconstruction. This rich and varied history is today reflected by a built environment that is defined as much by its stately mansions as it is by its modest cottages. Each tells a chapter in Beaufort's history.

This ninth edition of <u>A Guide to Historic Beaufort</u> represents a major revision to what has become, since its original publication in 1970, the standard reference on Beaufort's historic architecture. A great deal of new information has come to light in the almost thirty years since the book was first published. Some of this new information found its way into successive editions of the Guide. By 1997, the Foundation decided the book needed revision once again. With financial assistance from Beaufort County's Accommodations Tax program, work was begun on the present edition. In 1997 and 1998, the Foundation participated in a major new architectural inventory of the city and county. The inventory, completed by Brockington Associates, Inc. in association with Brooker Architectural Design Consultants, Historic Beaufort Foundation, and Preservation Consultants, Inc., identified that the historical record of many of Beaufort's notable buildings was often incomplete and in some cases it was inaccurate. In addition, little information had previously been available for many of the smaller scale residences throughout the historic district, or for many of the commercial buildings along Bay Street. Many of the photographs in this edition of the Guide were produced by the survey and are reprinted with the permission of the South Carolina Department of archives and history.

Information gathered during the inventory has improved the historical record of the city, but more work remains to be done. Historic Beaufort Foundation is continually working to document the city's rich architectural history and our understanding of the district and its buildings will continue to evolve. As new information becomes available, it will be incorporated into future editions of this book. We welcome inquiries from the public and the donation of documentation regarding any historic buildings within Beaufort County.

As you explore Beaufort's history and architecture, please keep in mind that most of its historic buildings are privately owned. Those who live, work, and are the stewards of these properties welcome your interest and appreciate your respect of their privacy.

Historic Beaufort

When visitors arrive in Beaufort, they are enchanted by the beauty of this small city, tucked off the beaten path on the banks of the intracoastal waterway. Historically however, Beaufort was not always so isolated. Over its 400 year history, Beaufort and the surrounding area have been witness to and a part of many of this nation's important events.

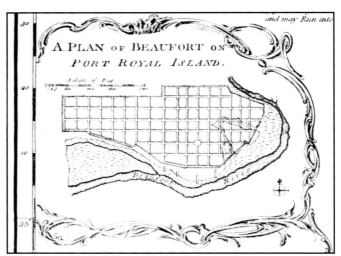
Beaufort in the 1770s.

In 1520, scarcely 30 years after Columbus landed in the New Wold, a Spanish explorer from Hispaniola sailed into Port Royal Sound and named the area Santa Elena. For almost 200 years following, the Spanish, French and English battled over this whole territory in an effort to colonize what they felt was a strategic location in the New World.

Colonial Beginnings

By the 1700s English planters and traders had firmly established a foothold in the Beaufort area. The site of Beaufort was probably begun as a British outpost as early as 1706 when a block house is thought to have been built near the river to protect inland passage. In 1710 the Lords Proprietors agreed that a seaport town should be erected on the sea islands. The new settlement was planned for a strategic point near the confluence of two tidal streams and was named Beaufort Town in honor of one of the Lords Proprietors, Henry Somerset, Duke of Beaufort.

The original town plan was made up of 397 lots and featured two points of focus. One was the bay, on which faced the front lots which were apparently the first to be laid out. The other was a square at the intersection of Carteret and Craven streets where land was reserved for public use. At that time, Charles and Duke streets were the western and northern boundaries of the town.

The original town plan was similar in concept to the Grand Modell of Charles Town (Charleston), some 40 years older. That plan in turn was patterned after such 17th-century English towns established in Ireland as Portarlington and Londonderry. The development of Beaufort was delayed by the Yemassee War in 1715 in which many of the Lowcountry Indian tribes, led by the Yemassee and angered by abuse from English traders, rose in revolt. The young town of Beaufort was attacked and many of the settlers were tortured and killed. A fortunate few managed to escape to a ship anchored in the bay. The rebellion was crushed and the Yemassee took refuge in Spanish Florida. The surviving planters returned to their burned-out homes and rebuilt. There were soon 70 families reported to be living in the area.

Initially, naval stores and provision crops were the economic mainstay of the Beaufort area. Later the main sources of wealth were shipping and agricultural exports. The largest fortunes were made in trade. South Carolina provided some of the largest private fortunes in America as well as the highest per capita income on the continent. Many of the prominent merchants were French Hugenots, including Jean delaGaye, Daniel DeSaussure, and John Mark Verdier

Although rice was an important export, the favored cash crop during the colonial period became the cultivation of indigo, from which blue dye was derived. Beaufort also became an important port of entry for the expanded trade in African slaves. The increased population in the area and the expansion of indigo production in the vicinity had accelerated the demand for slave labor. By 1763, Beaufort had a collector of the port and other customs officers. Shipbuilding was an important industry and was centered along Bay Street and on Black's Point in the present-day Point neighborhood.

By the eve of the Revolution, the population of Beaufort had increased to approximately 4,000 and an unidentified English traveler in 1774 saw Beaufort as "a well peopled good-looking town, better than half the size of Charlestown."

The Revolution

At that time, the people of Beaufort had many ties to England through trade and society. Wealthy local merchants and planters frequently visited London and sent their sons to England for their education. Many were loyal to the Crown. However, the misjudgment of George III's government in greatly increasing taxes, crippling the Province's economy and in ignoring constitutional rights, brought many locals to the Revolution. When the British governor Lord Charles Greville Montagu moved the seat of the Provincial Assembly from Charleston to Beaufort, seeking to gain control over the restive legislators, he sealed the doom of the royal cause. This event was listed by Thomas Jefferson as one of the grievances in the Declaration of Independence.

Beaufort played no major role in the early years of the Revolution, but as British hopes for success faded in New York and Pennsylvania they looked southward. In December 1778, the British captured and occupied Savannah. Early in the new year, General Augustine Prevost sent the ship HMS Vigilant with two hundred and fifty troops aboard to capture Beaufort. They landed at Laurel Bay and marched toward the town but were intercepted and turned back near the present Marine Corps Air Station by General William Moultrie and three hundred militia. The next month Prevost attempted, with near success, to capture Charleston but was forced to retreat down the coast, finally occupying Beaufort in July 1779. There was intermittent fighting in the area until 1782 when the British finally evacuated South Carolina. A number of prominent colonial Beaufortonians who remained loyal to the crown were compelled to leave the area, never to return. Among them were Lieutenant Gonernor William Bull, Jr. Beaufort continued to be important politically after the Revolution. The Beaufort planters joined their counterparts in Charleston and the other Lowcountry parishes in dominating the new state legislature, the General Assembly. The Lowcountry Federalists were responsible for the affirmative vote of the South Carolina ratification convention of 1788, in which South Carolina, as a key state, played a crucial role in the adoption of the present United States Constitution.

Beaufort Prospers

There was a brief period of economic depression following the Revolution but by the 1790s Beaufort had rebounded due to technical innovations such as the invention of the cotton gin and the introduction of a new crop, sea island cotton, the finest and most expensive cotton grown in America.

Beaufort was expanded again in the early nineteenth century by the incorporation of Black's Point, to the east of East Street, into the town. In 1809 the new boundaries of the town were defined as Hamer Street, Boundary Street, and the channel of Port Royal River.

The Stoney House (later the Sea Island Inn) was built as a summer home for one of Beaufort's most wealthy antebellum planters, Dr. George M. Stoney. This unusually large home was converted for use as an inn after the Civil War. It was demolished in 1959.

This was to be the greatest era of prosperity and influence in the town's long history. In the years between 1790 and 1860 cotton produced so many men of wealth and influence that one historian described Beaufort as "the wealthiest, most aristocratic and cultivated town of its size in America: a town, which though small in number of inhabitants, produced statesmen, scholars, sailors and divines, whose names and fame are known throughout the country." Some of Beaufort's more prominent citizens in the antebellum era were Senator Robert W. Barnwell, Secretary of the Navy Paul Hamilton, Congressman and Poet William J. Grayson, and Senator Robert Barnwell Rhett, the "Father of Secession."

This was the period when many of the fine homes which give distinction to Beaufort's National Historic District were built. The houses were surrounded by verdant gardens. An English geologist, Sir Charles Lyell, who visited Beaufort in 1845, gave an idyllic description of: "...a picturesque...assemblage of villas, the summer residences of numerous planters.... Each villa is shaded by a verandah, surrounded by beautiful live oaks and orange trees laden with fruit.... The Pride-of-India tree, with its berries now ripe, is an exotic much in favor here." The expansive grounds of the planters' residences also included numerous outbuildings, among them kitchens, carriage houses, stables and servants' quarters. During this period also, Beaufort gained the reputation for having some of the finest libraries and the best preparatory schools in the South. The most notable of these was the Beaufort College whose building, erected in 1852, now houses the branch campus of the University of South Carolina.

Beaufort society was the center of an elite class of planters from the surrounding country who moved to town for the summer because of the sickly atmosphere of the low-lying plantations during that season. Some prominent families lived in Beaufort all year. The planters followed the favored pursuits of the English country gentry. In addition to horse racing, hunting and fishing, a male favorite pastime was to assemble to "to eat, drink and talk of politics and planting."

Beaufort in the eighteenth and nineteenth centuries was certainly no outpost. The merchants and planters of Beaufort maintained close ties with Charleston and other Lowcountry communities. Charleston continued to be a frequent destination for the Beaufort area planters for family gatherings, shopping, consultations with factors and attorneys and for the winter social season. The mode of transportation at the time was by sailing schooner along the coast, by canoes along the network of Lowcountry tidal rivers, or by horseback and carriage along the roads. Later the steamboat and the railroad made travel faster and more comfortable.

Politically, South Carolina continued to be nationally important into the 19th century. Beaufort was no exception as it played an active role in the secession movement. Two prominent Beaufortonians, Robert Barnwell Rhett and William Ferguson Hutson, served on the seven member committee charged with drafting the Ordinance of Secession at the Secession Conference held in Charleston in December 1860. The political conflict came to its ultimate end when the Ordinance of Secession was signed December 20, 1860.

Union troops led into Beaufort by General Stevens on December 5, 1861
Engraving from Frank Leslie's Illustrated Newspaper

The Civil War

The Civil War once again focused attention on the strategic importance of Beaufort. The Federal government needed a base on the Atlantic coast for military operations and to blockade the Confederate ports. They decided that Beaufort was the ideal location for these purposes. In addition, the loss of Beaufort, at the center of a rich region, would be a destructive blow to the Confederacy.

The Verdier House, Photographed circa 1863, was in use as a post headquarters for occupying Federal Troops.

On November 7, 1861, a Federal fleet commanded by Commodore Samuel Francis DuPont, convoying a force of 12,000 men under Gen. Thomas W. Sherman, attacked and easily took Forts Walker (on Hilton Head Island) and Beauregard (on Bay Point Island) located on opposite sides of the Beaufort River at the entrance to the Port Royal harbor. The sea islands and the town of Beaufort were evacuated by the majority of the white inhabitants who abandoned plantations and town houses, leaving behind most of their slaves and literally half-eaten meals on the table. Noah Brooks, a war correspondent, referred to it as "The Grand Skedaddle."

Plantations and town properties were seized as abandoned lands by the Federal authorities and many were sold to recoup the Direct Tax. The town was resurveyed into newly numbered blocks and lots, and given new alphabetical and numerical names to the streets. About one-third of the land in Beaufort and the surrounding occupied area was sold at auction to Northern buyers, many of whom were speculators. The remainder was acquired at auction by the United States government and was used as military headquarters, barracks, stables, stores and hospitals. Other properties were offered for sale to the freedmen.

During the war, Beaufort's African-American population began to grow as refugees from nearby plantations made their way to town looking for shelter and work. At first classified as contraband of war, but later freed in 1863 by the Emancipation Proclamation, these former slaves took part in the first efforts to assimilate freed blacks into the broader society known as the Port Royal experiment. With the establishment of schools such as the Penn School on St. Helena Island and the Mather School on Port Royal Island, freedmen were given access to educational opportunities. Redistribution of land resulting from the Direct Tax allowed many former slaves to be able to purchase land for the first time.

611 Bay Street during Union Occupation, 1860s. Building lost in 1907 by fire.

After the War

The war brought about profound social and political changes in the city. Beaufort's population shifted from a white majority to an African-American one. Prior to the war, there were approximately 850 white residents, a number that fell to 466 by the time of the 1870 census. Conversely, the community's African-American population rose dramatically after the war, reaching 1,273 by 1870. With this majority, Beaufort's African-American community was able to gain substantial political influence.

Largely because of its early occupation, the confiscation of the property of the former plantation owners, and the establishment of schools during the war, blacks in Beaufort County enjoyed better access to education and property than in many parts of the post-war south. As a result, it became somewhat of a haven for African-Americans during Reconstruction. Black population in the city rose in part as people moved from surrounding counties to avail themselves of the more favorable political and social climate.

Bay Street - street scene during the 1940s.

Historic Beaufort Foundation created its revolving fund in the 1970s to preserve endangered historic buildings

African-Americans during this time resided throughout the city. The more prominent blacks acquired the mansions of former slaveholders. Others built new dwellings scattered within the city's existing neighborhoods. Still others began to acquire property and to build houses within the Northwest Quadrant neighborhood, an area that had largely been undeveloped before the war. An 1878 article in <u>Harper's New Monthly Magazine</u>, stated that most of the city's African-Americans occupied "their former slave quarters or new and neat shanties or houses."

By the 1870s Beaufort had greatly improved its economic situation. Much of the postwar economic recovery of the Lowcountry was due to the introduction and development of phosphate mining in the late 1860s. Sea Island cotton cultivation was also revived although to a more limited extent than before, as was rice planting. The 1870 census listed 20 merchants in various trades, 21 grocers, a banker, and a restauranteur. By 1883 there were 43 stores in Beaufort. During the postbellum period, Beaufort also became a winter resort for Northerners. The tourists were lured by promotional publications which praised the healthy warm winter climate and the opportunities for hunting and fishing. Wealthy northerners such as Harry Payne Whitney, William K. Vanderbilt and others all owned winter homes in the area. In addition, the continued strategic importance of Beaufort led the United States government to maintain the Port Royal Naval Station and also established the U.S. Marine Corps Post on Parris Island in 1891.

With a return to prosperity and a rise in the population came a crippling blow when a horrendous hurricane struck the area in 1893. The hurricane came ashore at high tide, completely covering the sea islands. Many thousands were drowned, numerous buildings in the town were damaged, and the local phosphate mining industry was destroyed.

Beaufort's fortune was soon to turn once again for the better with the advent of truck farming which became Beaufort's next important industry, replacing cotton and rice. The agricultural prosperity brought a renewed confidence to the town of Beaufort and an increased effort was made to boost tourism with some of the large antebellum mansions turned into guest houses. Tourism, the seafood industry including the canning of shrimp and oysters, and truck farming remained the most important economic activities throughout the first half of this century. The tourist trade continued to grow as did employment from Parris Island. In 1940, Beaufort was once again ravaged by a hurricane but survived and was rebuilt.

Today, light manufacturing, military installations, and tourism bring in new dollars. Retirees and young families, drawn by climate, history, and the as-yet-unspoiled beauty, are the new settlers who add to the intellectual and cultural life of the sea islands. The town, in the words of the Federal Writers Program of 1940 continues to be "a monument to endurance."

Beaufort's Architecture

Beaufort's 304-acre National Historic Landmark District retains a rich and diverse collection of historic architecture. While noted for the elegant landmarks of its wealthy plantation past, the city also retains significant buildings reflecting the continuum of its rich history and the cultural and economic diversity of its population. When carefully observed, the full range of the city's history and its changing patterns of development unfold to the eye. The relationship between these buildings and their natural setting is ever-present, as the water that surrounds three sides of the city remains a principal character defining element of the district. Moss draped oaks, palmettos, crepe myrtles, and other native plant materials help to complete the picture, as do manmade landscapes, both formal and informal.

Contrasting the early architectural character of Charleston, Savannah and Beaufort, architectural historians Carl Feiss and Russell Wright, who conducted the first historic inventory of Beaufort in 1968-1969, noted: "It is a remarkable fact that these neighboring three communities, developing simultaneously, should have each so successfully created their own high quality, individual architectural design." Where Charleston and Savannah architecture was urban in character, reflecting the status of each as important cities, Beaufort's character was quite different. As Feiss and Wright described it, "Beaufort's houses, free standing on large lots, are more akin to the architecture of the Southern plantations of the period, plantations brought into town, than anything found in

The Verdier House, 801 Bay Street. Representative of high style Beaufort architecture of the Federal period.

801 Duke Street - A simple vernacular cottage typical of many in the historic district.

Charleston or Savannah."The earliest settlers in Beaufort, Barbadian planters, English indentured servants, tradesmen, and religious dissenters, came here to seek their fortunes beginning in 1710. The houses they built have largely disappeared over time. Perhaps the earliest house to survive and give indication of the appearance of this period of Beaufort's architecture is the Thomas Hepworth House. Often reported to have been constructed as early as 1717, the house has been altered over time. Still, it continues to be representative of Beaufort's colonial period. Only a few additional buildings dating from before the Revolutionary War have been documented in the city. Among those thought to be of this period are the John Chaplin House at 712 New Street, the Elizabeth Hext House at 207 Hancock Street, and the DeSaussure Store at 715 Bay Street.

As prosperity increased, Beaufort's houses grew larger and more elaborate. Designed for airiness and coolness, the houses typically faced south and had wide verandas. Many of the most prominent houses were built close to the water, as the water was the principal entrance to the city and afforded the best breezes. Buildings were typically constructed of wood. Tabby and brick were commonly used for foundations, although many buildings were built entirely of these materials.

Tabby

Tabby is an important local building material, as its components are indigenous to the coast. A durable cement-like material, tabby was made of oyster shells, sand, and lime (obtained through the burning of oyster shells) pounded into reusable wooden forms. Once relatively common in Beaufort where it was used in fortifications, houses, stores and a variety of out-buildings, tabby is now represented by a handful of structures, including the Barnwell-Gough House, Tabby Manse, and the Saltus House, although many foundations and vestiges of walls remain.

*Tabby Ruins of the Talbird House on Hancock Street
as photographed in the 1940s*

Beaufort National Historic Landmark District

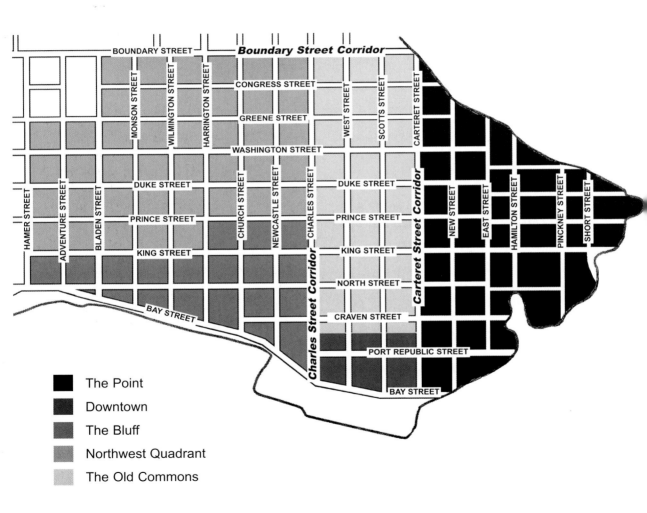

The Point
Downtown
The Bluff
Northwest Quadrant
The Old Commons

Buildings in the National Historic Landmark district exhibit many of the principal historic styles of American architecture from Colonial to modern. Still, few represent "pure" examples of any one style and stylistic influences are often mixed. As Beaufort's prosperity rose and fell, new buildings were built and older buildings were often remodeled. The result is a rich architectural tapestry, the character of which is visually dominated by a relatively limited number of antebellum mansions set among numerous smaller scale late-19th to early-20th century buildings. Architectural character changes from neighborhood to neighborhood and often block to block. The city's earliest and grandest buildings are generally located on The Point and along The Bluff. The architecture of the Old Commons Neighborhood is more eclectic, with both large mansions and small cottages dating from all periods of the city's history. The Northwest Quadrant, which developed after the Civil War, is much different in character, as its folk style buildings are typically small in scale and simple in detail. Beaufort's small downtown commercial district retains vestiges of its mixed commercial and residential use in the Colonial and antebellum periods, although its present commercial character is more a product of its later Victorian and 20th century commercial buildings.

For more information about architectural styles commonly found in Beaufort, please consult The Beaufort Preservation Manual (1979, John Milner Associates) and Beaufort County Above Ground Historic Resources (1998, Brockington and others). A more general guide to America's historic architecture is A Field Guide to American Houses (1984, McAlester).

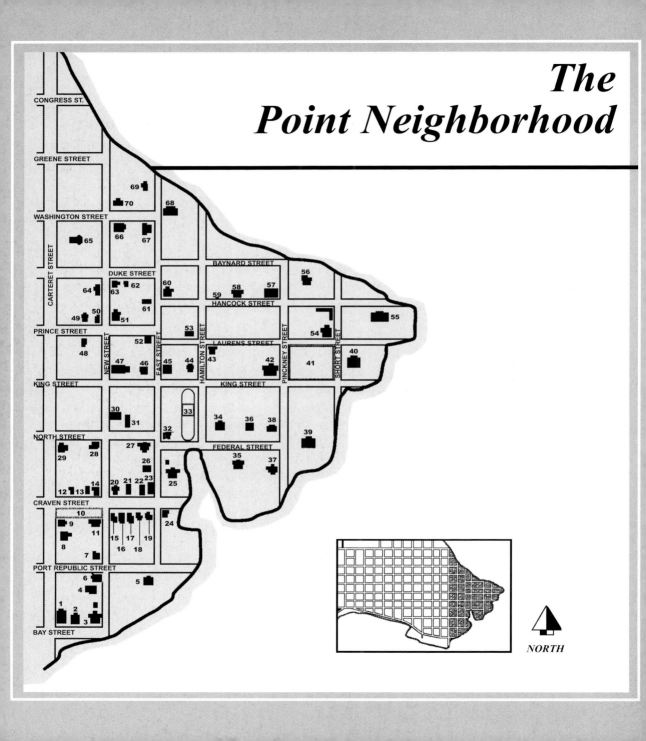

The Point Neighborhood

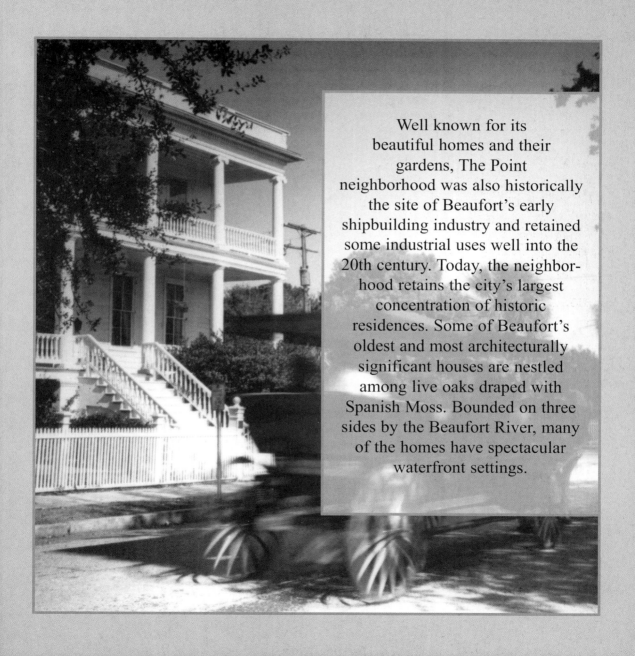

Well known for its beautiful homes and their gardens, The Point neighborhood was also historically the site of Beaufort's early shipbuilding industry and retained some industrial uses well into the 20th century. Today, the neighborhood retains the city's largest concentration of historic residences. Some of Beaufort's oldest and most architecturally significant houses are nestled among live oaks draped with Spanish Moss. Bounded on three sides by the Beaufort River, many of the homes have spectacular waterfront settings.

1. *Wallace House*
611 Bay Street
1907

The Fuller family once owned a large circa 1800 Federal-style tabby mansion on this site. That house was destroyed in the great Beaufort fire of 1907. The present structure was built prior to 1912 and has excellent Victorian millwork typical of the period.

2. 607 Bay Street
William Joseph Thomas House
1909

An eighteenth-century tabby house built by a member of the Elliott family originally stood on this site. This house was torn down and replaced by a clapboard dwelling which burned in the fire of 1907. The present house was built in 1909 and is a fine solid Victorian structure. William Joseph Thomas had it built of patterned concrete blocks that were made near the house from special materials brought by boat from Charleston.

3. *601 Bay Street*

Lewis Reeve Sams House
1852

This handsome Beaufort Style house has excellent exterior woodwork, Ionic columns over Doric on the verandahs, fine doorways and chimneys, and marble front stairs. The interior includes black marble mantels and excellent plaster work. Construction circa 1852 is attributed to Lewis Reeve Sams (1784-1856), a planter who at one time owned half of Dataw Island. The Rev. Thomas Fuller Sams acquired the property after his mother's death in 1857 and is listed on 1862 Direct Tax records as being its owner on the eve of the Union occupation, during which the house was used as Hospital #14. Sams was able to reacquire the house after the war, mortgaging it to George W. Woodman in 1867 and to George Waterhouse in 1868. Waterhouse, a native of Lyman, Maine, came to Beaufort in 1864 and operated a store on Bay Street, soon becoming a prominent business and civic leader. He purchased the house from Sams in 1869. According to local tradition, the house survived the great fire of 1907 by the efforts of the Waterhouse cotton gin workers, who formed a bucket brigade and used wet blankets to beat out the flames. The small one-room house in the back yard is thought to have been used as a wash house.

4. *212 New Street*

William Waterhouse House
1907

A Sanborn Insurance Company* map of 1899 does not show a house on this site, but the present house does appear on a 1912 map. A 1968 survey of historic sites in Beaufort indicates the house was built in 1907. Local tradition holds that the house was built by William Waterhouse for his wife. This typical late-Victorian style house has spacious piazzas on two sides. The upper piazzas were added later. This house has been converted for use as a bed and breakfast.

* *The Sanborn Company prepared very detailed maps for cities and towns across the country that were used for insurance purposes.*

5. 500 Port Republic Street
George Moss Stoney House
circa 1823; circa 1840

In the John Campbell painting of 1798 a house is shown on this lot. Purchased by Dr. George Moss Stoney, a physician, the earlier house was replaced to please his wife, Sarah Barnwell. Previous accounts have placed the construction of the house circa 1823, while visible details and Greek Revival motifs suggest either construction circa 1840 or a major rebuilding then. The District Tax Commission map of 1862 shows the house in the ownership of Mrs. S. B. Stoney. An exposed beam in the rear upper hall indicates that the house was originally one room deep. Also found in recent remodeling were hand-forged nails, mortised corners of clapboard and wooden pegs in sills. The present house is beautifully proportioned with upper and lower porches on three sides, each supported by fourteen Doric columns and each finished with denticulated trim on the rooflines.

6. *214 New Street*

Thomas Hepworth House
between 1717 and 1722; possibly rebuilt circa 1760

This house has long been referred to as the oldest house in Beaufort with a construction date of 1717 cited. This date may be far too early, with stylistic evidence suggesting a construction, or reconstruction, date of circa 1760. It is documented that Thomas Hepworth, Chief Justice of the Colony, acquired an original grant for the property in 1717 that carried a stipulation that a house be built within five years. Hepworth sold the property to Thomas Burton in 1741. Subsequent owners included the Barnwell, Deveaux, and Johnson families. Writing in 1871 of the War of Revolution as it affected Beaufort, Dr. John A. Johnson stated: "The only remaining memorials of that war within our present view are the two redoubts in the north western suburbs and the little Dutch house on the corner of Port Republic and New Streets." He continued: "At the close of the last century (eighteenth) an early cotton gin was invented and the first one was exhibited in the large front parlor of the antiquated Dutch-looking building at the south west corner of New and Port Republic Streets, to the moderns known as Republican Headquarters." In the early 1800s William Fickling conducted a private school for boys in this house. It later served as a meeting place for local Masons. During World War II, the house was converted into apartments. The house was restored to a single family residence by Mr. & Mrs. Somers Pringle in the 1950s. The house is a Colonial two-story cottage with a side porch. Its roof lines are simple gables broken by side dormer windows. A local tradition that ventilation piercings on the north side of the foundation were intended as rifle slots for defense against Indian attack is without documentation. The floor sills are hand hewn from whole trees adzed to 16 inches. The chimney is seven feet square set on a footing but finished to give the appearance of four chimneys. The origin of the attached stair tower to the south has not been established, but it is known the house was extended one bay to the east (toward New Street) between 1884 and 1899.

7. 601 Port Republic Street
Pre Civil War

This charming small house is probably one of the oldest in town. The property on which it stands was first granted Auqust 8, 1717 to Francis La Basseur. In 1759 Philip Martinangele owned it. During the Civil War it was sold at the tax sale of 1863 for one hundred dollars. The quaint white clapboard house was originally two rooms deep, upstairs and down, and has been enlarged by the addition of a wing in the rear.

8. *305 Carteret Street*

This house was built circa 1910. The 1905 Sanborn Insurance map does not show this structure but it is shown in its present configuration in the 1912 edition. Major George Osterhout, U. S. Marine Corps, owned the house in the early-20th century. Osterhout, a member of the Parris Island class of 1909, served in World War I and later returned to Beaufort. In the 1920s, he participated in archaeological investigations on Parris Island then thought to have identified the site of the 1562 French settlement Charlesfort.

9. *311 Carteret Street*
John F. Morrall House circa 1916

The Sanborn Insurance Company maps do not show building on this site in 1912, but this structure was present in1924. The property was acquired by A. S. Morrall in April 1913. Morrall in turn transferred ownership to his son W. M. Morrall on 31 January 1916. No house is mentioned in either deed. In March 1919, W. M. Morrall sold the property "with dwelling and houses thereon" to his brother John F. Morrall, a Beaufort trader and local historian whose family retained it until 1997.

10. *Corner of Carteret and Craven Streets*
Morrall Park
eighteenth century

When the town of Beaufort was first laid out, its principal streets were Carteret and Craven Streets. A town square was set aside at their intersection. Each of its four corners was reserved for public use and remained so until well into the nineteenth century. This lot remains as the last open corner of the original town square and is now used as a park.

11. *310 New Street*
Berners Barnwell Sams House
1818

Built by Dr. Berners Barnwell Sams in 1818, this white clapboard house was originally in the Federal style and had a two-story portico centered on its facade. Later, the rear wing was added and the house was remodeled in the Greek Revival style. The full-width porch was added at that time, as were parapets which have since been lost. During the Civil War the house was used as Contraband Hospital No. 10. The term Contraband was used to refer to former slaves within areas occupied by federal troops.

12.-14. *601, 603 and 609 Craven Street*
circa 1890

This section of Craven Street has become one of the most charming parts of old Beaufort. Many of the houses along this block and on the block to the east were built in the 1880s and 1890s in similar Victorian styles. Several are almost identical. All have decorations made by wood working machinery newly invented in the late nineteenth-century. Several have turrets and towers; some have colored glass; most have decorative spindles; a number have bay windows; several have nice piazzas.

Sanborn Insurance Company maps indicate that these houses were erected sometime between 1884 and 1894, during which time the entire south side of Block 36 underwent redevelopment. Previously occupied by a meat market and jail in 1884, E. A Scheper purchased the strip of land fronting on Craven Street in December 1892. He divided it into four lots and built four Victorian houses by 1894, as indicated on the Sanborn map of that year. Of these houses, only the three at 601, 603, and 609 Craven Street remain.

12. 601 Craven Street

13. 603 Craven Street

14. 609 Craven Street

15. 510 Craven Street

16. 508 Craven Street

17. 506 Craven Street

15.-17. *506, 508 and 510 Craven Street*
circa 1880

George Holmes purchased these lots from George A. Springer in 1876. Holmes, who resided on North Street, is thought to have built these three houses circa 1880. During World War II, the upstairs of 508 Craven Street was converted into apartments for Marines stationed in Beaufort. The house was returned to use as a single family dwelling after the Korean War.

18.-19. *502 and 504 Craven Street*
circa 1880

This pair of very similar houses is first shown on the Sanborn Insurance Company map of 1899.

18. 502 Craven Street

19. 504 Craven Street

20. *509 Craven Street*
Adam Davis Hare House
circa 1924

Adam Davis Hare acquired the property in May 1919 and is said to have built the present house circa 1924 on the foundation of a mid-nineteenth century house that had been destroyed by fire. In the 1950s the property was purchased and altered extensively. From condemned eighteenth and nineteenth-century Savannah residences came ceiling moldings, window frames, mantels, and lumber. Bricks to buttress existing foundations were purchased from the Trenholm School in Charleston, and Robert E. Marvin of Walterboro was commissioned to design a parterre garden behind the house using bricks from the old Savannah City Market, then being demolished.

21. *507 Craven Street*

circa 1880

Of the several Victorian houses along this section of Craven Street, 507 Craven exhibits more elaborate details than the others. The 1899 Sanborn Insurance map shows the present two story main structure with a front stoop but no porch. By 1924, the side porch had been added.

21. 507 Craven Street

22. 503 Craven Street

22-23. *503 and 501 Craven Street*

These two Victorian houses were built by E. A. Scheper circa 1886.

23. 501 Craven Street

24. *400 Craven Street* (historically 311 East Street)
Lambeth House
circa 1820

The original house was constructed prior to the Civil War, although the original builder and date of construction are not known. Early Beaufort land records indicate the first owner may have been John E. Lambeth, with construction occurring about 1820. John E. and Susan F. Lambeth transferred the property to their son Daniel J. Lambeth in 1855. Lambeth was able to reacquire the property after the Civil War, retaining ownership until 1875. Prominent local merchant George Waterhouse owned the house from 1875 until 1893, when it was reportedly sold to the Danner family. The house underwent extensive remodeling in 1985-1990, which included construction of a substantial addition to the east and the loss of the original "T" form of the house.

25. *411 Craven Street*

Joseph Johnson House, The Castle
1861

The Castle was built for Dr. Joseph Fickling Johnson by J. S. Cooper, a local builder, according to an agreement signed December 5, 1859. The contracted work was completed by August 8, 1861, however some elements of the house, notably its porch railings, mantelpieces, and ironwork are reported to have been caught in the Union naval blockade and never reached the site. Bricks for the house are reported to have been made on Dr. Johnson's Lady's Island plantation near Brickyard Point. The house was confiscated during the Civil War and became part of Hospital #6. Dr. Johnson, unlike many of Beaufort's pre-war residents, was able to reacquire the house at the end of the war upon payment of $2,000 in taxes. The house remained in Johnson's family until 1981. The house is Italian Renaissance in feeling and is said to be almost an exact copy of one in England, destroyed during World War II. Constructed on a crib of palmetto logs, the walls are of soft brick covered with a thin layer of plaster. The color is muted and changeable, in shades of gray, tan, and pink, subtly shifting with the light. Six massive columns support the double portico, with balusters between that enclose the upper and lower porches. The decorated parapet is five feet high, with four triple chimneys towering above it. Long French windows, some of the seventy-nine windows in the house, flank the front doors, upstairs and down. Some of the original mantels have been replaced by Regency ones rescued from an old Beaufort house being demolished. The house, one of the most photographed in America, occupies a full city block and is set amid lush gardens with hundreds of azaleas and camellias. It faces a great bend in the Beaufort River, and giant live oaks guard the front and back. Many of the specimen trees and shrubs in the garden were planted by Dr. Johnson, including a pair of ancient

olive trees, brought from the Mount of Olives in the Holy Land. A former director of the National Trust for Historic Preservation called it "One of the great houses of the South Carolina coast." He spoke of "the extraordinary grandeur of the almost medieval house . . . its air of somber mystery, set in great oaks at the water's edge."

26. *406 East Street*
circa 1886

Built by E. A. Scheper circa 1886 the house is one of three almost identical structures, the others are 503 and 501 Craven Street. The house was inherited by Agnes S. Eubank who sold it to Eliza J. McKee in 1918.

27. *412 East Street*
Henry Farmer House
circa 1810

This early nineteenth-century house with double galleries set on a high tabby foundation once overlooked the Beaufort River across the lot where The Castle now stands. Henry Farmer sold his house to a widow, Charlotte Beadon. Mrs. Beadon was involved in a law suit over Cat Island, and Richard Fuller acted as her lawyer, winning both the case and the widow. The Fullers were both lovers of flowers, and when Dr. Fuller travelled abroad in the 1830s he returned with a number of imported specimens for their garden, most notably the Roman laurel and Guernsey lily (nerine), along with an Italian marble mantel for the drawing room. He built the lace brick wall around the house and enclosed the upper portion of the double portico for use as an upstairs study, where he pursued his varied vocations. During the Civil War the house was used as a Federal hospital.

28. *414 New Street*
William Johnson House
circa 1776

Construction of this house is attributed to William Johnson circa 1776. Architectural details suggest this construction date is likely, although a somewhat earlier building date cannot be ruled out. The site was owned before the Civil War by W. C. Danner. Samuel J. Bampfield purchased the property from Samuel Green in 1877. Bampfield, born in 1849 to free Black parents, was editor of the Beaufort New South, a weekly newspaper; served as a state representative, from 1874 to 1876; held the office of clerk of court for Beaufort County for twenty years; and was appointed postmaster in 1897. After his death in 1899, his widow Elizabeth Lydia Smalls, daughter of Robert Smalls, succeeded him as postmaster and held the post until her retirement in 1908. Bampfield sold this property shortly before his death to George Holmes.

29. *409 Carteret Street*
nineteenth century

This house is thought to have been constructed as a one-room deep two-story dwelling in the 1830s or 1840s. It is located on property originally granted to John Barnwell on July 18, 1764. A small house on this lot is said to have been either remodeled or replaced by the present house. The 1863 Direct Tax sale map shows that the property was purchased by a Rickenbacker for $600. After the war, possibly about 1880, the house was more than doubled in size, with additional rooms being added to the rear and the entire building re-roofed. Interior changes were made during the 1920s and again in the 1950s or 1960s when the house, now offices, became a ladies shop.

30. *509 North Street*
Thomas Hazel House
circa 1850

This house is often reported to have been built in 1852 by Thomas Hazel as a "honeymoon cottage" for his bride. It is one of only a few in Beaufort which retains its original parapet. George Holmes, who married Mr. Hazel's daughter, bought the house soon after it was built. During the Civil War, it was used as a hospital. In 1902, Captain John Foster bought the property at an auction. The house has three garret windows above the second level verandah and handsome marble mantels in the interior.

31. *507 North Street*
Gustave Sanders House
circa 1875

It is not known who built this Victorian house in the late nineteenth century, but Gustave Sanders bought it in 1903 and members of his family owned it until 1998. The double front piazzas are supported by Doric-style columns. Victorian trim is found under the piazza eaves and on the double bay windows. There are arched glass panels with sidelights around the front door.

32. 409 Federal Street
Joseph Hazel House
circa 1840

Documentary evidence suggests this house was built for Joseph Hazel, a local landowner, planter and plantation manager with property on Lady's Island. Dale Rosengarten, in his book <u>Tombee</u>, remarked that Hazel "was a highly successful grower of sea island cotton." The house, along with the former Joseph Johnson house to the south, formed Union Hospital #6 during the Civil War. Redeemed after the Civil War, the property remained in the Hazel Family until the death of Joseph Hazel's grand-daughter Francis Fleming (Fannie) Hazel in 1936. Subsequently, the house was extensively altered, especially at its south facade. In 1989, the alterations were removed and much of the original exterior appearance of the house was restored.

33. *Tidal Basin*
Corner of Federal and Hamilton Streets

This tidal basin extending north from Federal Street to King Street occupies the eastern half of Block 18. It is a remnant of larger body of tidal water which in 1862 extended right and left along what is now King Street.

34. *315 Federal Street*
circa 1840 ;1893

Local tradition has often cited John Bythewood as the builder of this house in the early 1800s. Architectural evidence suggests a later construction date. Prior to the Civil War, the lot was owned by Ann B. Oswald and her sister Margaret (Mary) R. Bell, daughters of Bythewood. In 1862, Margaret testified she had lived in the house for "20 years before" outbreak of Civil War. Conveyed after the Direct Tax sale by Tax Sale Certificate #223, the house is said to have been bought by a former slave of Mary Bell. The house remained in the hands of former slaves and their descendants until it was severely damaged and abandoned after the storm of 1893. Stories attached to the house suggest that during the great storm boatloads of refugees from the islands were unloaded on the front porch, the highest point in the vicinity. It sat abandoned until 1898, when it was purchased and restored by H. T. Danner. Of the original Adam-style mantels, only one remains to suggest the former character of the house. Golden oak mantels, installed after the storm have recently been replaced by fine Adam-style mantels and ceiling cornices salvaged from a house which stood formerly at the corner of Charles and King Streets. The size of the foundation beams, pegged rafters, and hand-made nails show the unusual soundness and age of the construction.

35. *310 Federal Street*
circa 1892

A house thought to have been constructed on this site in the late eighteenth century by John Bell is shown on a 1798 painting of Beaufort by John Barnwell Campbell. It was later owned by Senator Robert Woodward Barnwell (1801-1882). At the time of the US Direct Tax Commission auction during the Civil War, the house was used as a hospital. This early house burned in the 1890s. The present house was built on the tabby foundation of the original house and has been attributed to a Dr. Prioleau. A photograph showing the house after the 1893 hurricane indicates that the present house had been constructed by that time. The house is typical of many older Beaufort homes, with a central hallway and lower and upper porches on its south elevation.

36. *309 Federal Street*
circa 1902

This house is reported to have been constructed for the Burns family, who owned the property from 1902 until 1920. It was later owned by Sampson Paul (1920-1932) and Casper Farbstein (1932-1980).

37. *302 Federal Street*

William Fripp House, "Tidewater"
circa 1830

This superbly designed, well-proportioned house was built in approximately 1830 and is attributed to William Fripp (1788-1860), one of area's wealthiest nineteenth-century planters. Its two-story portico faces the river, and the excellent interior boasts a fan transom, a Palladian window, period mantels and molded plaster work. William Fripp was the son of Captain John Fripp and Martha Scott Fripp. A family sketch of William by a great-grandson, Frampton Ellis of Atlanta, says this: "He was a polished scholar, an extensive traveler, and a thoroughly Christian gentleman. He was generous and open-hearted, a large part of his income being set aside for the poor of his county. In fact, so well known were his benevolences and purity of life that he was known all over the state as 'Good Billy Fripp.'" William Fripp married Sarah Harriett Reynolds Prentiss, a widow with many possessions, in May 1820. At the time of his death, Fripp is reported to have owned more than 3,000 acres of land on St. Helena Island, encompassing nine plantations and 313 Negro slaves.The Fripp family is documented as having owned the property at the time of the Direct Tax auction of 1862. Subsequent to the war, a tax claim was filed by his wife Sarah H. Fripp and daughter Juliana Prioleau. The house was acquired in 1936 by W. Brantley Harvey, Sr., a prominent Beaufort attorney who served in the South Carolina Senate. It remained in the Harvey family until 1997.

38. *303 Federal Street* *historic view*

James Rhett House
circa 1886

James Rhett acquired this property in October 1885 and is the probable builder of the present house. It is likely that work commenced shortly thereafter as a home for Rhett and his new bride in May 1886. On each floor a center hall separates two large front rooms with twelve-foot ceilings. The downstairs rooms have elaborate cast plaster moldings and ceiling medallions. An arcaded masonry wall supports double verandahs across the front of the house. Wide bay windows extend the width of the parlor on the west. Jib doors give access to the porches and also add cross ventilation. Folk tradition has long held that Rhett began his house in 1884 intending to make it two rooms deep and was later forced to change his plans for financial reasons. While this accounts for the name "Rhett's Folly" often associated with the house, no documentation has been found to substantiate the story.

39. *501 Pinckney Street*
James Robert Verdier House, "Marshlands"
circa 1814

"Marshlands" was built for Dr. James Robert Verdier, the second son of local merchant and planter John Mark Verdier I. Verdier was a pioneer in the the successful treatment of yellow fever. Owned by William Chisholm just before the Civil War, a Direct Tax claim was made after the Civil War in the name of Sarah P. Chisholm and Samuel A. Chisholm. The graceful waterfront home is set high off the ground and supported by arches. Inside, an Adam style motif prevails with the lovely mantels and the beautiful stairway lit by a Palladian window.

Note: (A waterfront view of 501 Pinckney Street
is pictured on the cover of this book.)

40. *100 Laurens Street*

Paul Hamilton House, "The Oaks"
circa 1855

This Italianate style house set in the shade of magnificent oaks is of frame construction on a brick foundation. The wide porches extend across the front of the house and continue around the sides to meet the projecting back rooms which have bay windows rising from the floor almost to the ceiling. The house has unusual carved mantels that extend around the sides of the chimneys. According to Direct Tax Case testimony, Colonel Paul Hamilton and his wife built this house "shortly" before the Civil War. Hamilton was the grandson of Paul Hamilton, Secretary of the Navy under President Madison. The family deserted the house in 1861 when Beaufort was occupied by Federal soldiers and it was used during the war as Union Hospital #1. Local tradition holds that when the house was auctioned in November 1865, Colonel Hamilton declared that he would bid up to a million dollars to save his home from becoming a school for Negroes. The Colonel obtained an option on the house with payment to be made within three days, this period allowing for a boat trip to Charleston to secure funds. On the second day, however, the Colonel's young son ran home with the news that the house would be sold at sunset. Mr. George Holmes, a northern merchant, led other indignant citizens in hastily raising the money before sunset and the house was bought in the name of Colonel Hamilton.

41. *"The Green"*
Bounded by Laurens, King, Pinckney, and Short Streets

"The Green" or "Front Green" is an open space long associated with the Berners Barnwell Sams House located at 201 Laurens Street to the northeast. The property was in the ownership of R.R. Sams just before the Civil War. During the war it was used as a military campground.

42. *604 Pinckney Street*
Edward Means House
1855-1857

Progress on the construction of this brick mansion between 1855 and 1857 is documented by surviving correspondence between Means and Franklin Talbird, who supervised its construction. On 13 December 1855 Talbird wrote: "The roof of your house is boarded and ready for the tinner..." and by 3 January 1857 he continued "the painter told me he would be finished in two weeks." A special war correspondent sent the following dispatch to the New York Daily Tribune in December, 1861: "The splendor of the houses and furniture and the beauty of the place may have been exaggerated, but the house of Colonel Edward Means would be called handsome in any town in the North." The house was used as Union Hospital #2 during the Civil War. Entered from the end elevation facing east on the "The Green," the interior of the house is notable for its spacious quality. It has fine woodwork, marble mantels, and a beautiful floating spiral staircase. Like most Beaufort antebellum houses, the porch faces south to receive prevailing breezes, sun in winter and shade in summer.

43. *321 King Street*
circa 1800

This house was owned by the Rhodes family prior to the Civil War. Members of the Rhodes family then included merchants, politicians, and planters. Architectural evidence suggests a construction date of between 1790 and 1815, but any attributed date requires confirmation.

44. *401 King Street*
"Little Taj"

This site belonged to the Rhodes family before the Civil War. In a conveyance dated 1860, John J. Rhodes refers to Block 17, on which the property is located, as "the Mill". The present house now looks out toward a tidal basin which before the Civil War was much larger than today, one channel then extending in front of the site to the east and west. The construction date most often cited for the property is 1856, however unconfirmed sources suggest it may have been standing in 1823 when a Miss Jane Bond was married from the house to Henry McKee, for whom 511 Prince Street (the Robert Smalls House) was built. A typical Beaufort small house, it was built to take full advantage of all breezes with porches at the front on both floors, and small wings to bring the breezes into the rear rooms. When a rear wall was cut into recently to relocate an air conditioner, it was found the corner supports of the house are unsawn limbs of trees about six inches in diameter. The name "Little Taj" appears to be a modern association referring to the reflection of the house in the tidal basin across the road

45. *411 King Street*

F. W. Sanders House
1910

Replacing a cottage that burned in the fire which swept through the town in 1907, the present two story house was built in 1910 of heart-pine with mahogany woodwork. Surrounded by a spacious lawn, the house has ten large rooms and six fireplaces which give it an air of gracious living.

46. *501 King Street*
William Wigg Barnwell House
circa 1816; moved 1973

As recently as January, 1973, this house was slated for demolition. Through the intervention of Historic Beaufort Foundation several stays were granted and in September, 1973, it was moved from its original location at the southwest corner of Prince and Scott Streets to its present site. The twelve-room town house is said to have been built by the Gibbes brothers on behalf of their sister, Sarah Reeve Gibbes, who married William Wigg Barnwell, grandson of the Revolutionary War hero, Major William Hazzard Wigg. During the Civil War, the house served as Union Hospital #4. The house remained in the Barnwell family until 1895, when the Barnwell's son Bower Williamson Barnwell died. The house later served as a school and as an apartment house. For most of this century it sustained much abuse and neglect. Despite this, much of the original paneling and a magnificent stairhall remained fairly intact. The house was purchased and restored by antiques dealer Jim Williams of Savannah, Georgia.

47. *601 New Street*
First African Baptist Church
circa 1861

This church is thought to have been built circa 1861 by the Baptist Church of Beaufort for its African American members. During the war, the black congregation formed a seperate church known as the First African Baptist Church. A marble plaque on the church states: "Presented as a token of respect by A. D. Deas to the first and present pastor, Reverend A. Waddell, of the First Baptist Church, a native of Savannah, Georgia, who became pastor of said church First of January 1865."

48. *608 Prince Street*
nineteenth century

On February 3, 1864 this house was sold at public auction by the United States Tax Commission for $450 to Hector Powell. The deed states that he "served as a volunteer in Company E, First South Carolina Volunteers, Army of the United States, for a full period of five months." This is the first record of the house. The original house had four rooms, each with a fireplace and heart pine floors. The fireplaces, floors, and two downstairs mantels are original. Several rooms were added during a substanttial remodeling of the house in 1977.

49. *605 Prince Street*
Pre Civil War

Late Greek Revival detailing at the entrance surround suggests this house was constructed during the 1850s. The "T" shaped plan is shown complete on the 1912 Sanborn Insurance map. The 1968 historic sites survey form states: "It was bought by a colored minister, Rev. Waddell, who served the African Baptist Church on King and East Streets." In 1925 it was bought by the Sanders family and then by the Cook family.

50. *601 Prince Street*
Washington House, circa 1850; 1912

The date of construction of this house is uncertain. Often noted as having been constructed by Julius I. Washington in 1912, recent renovation suggests that it may have actually been built in the 1840s or 1850s. Washington added the two rear upstairs rooms and reversed the stairs, so that they ascended from the rear of the central hall. The house is shown in this configuration on the 1912 Sanborn Map. The Washington family retained ownership until the 1960s.

51. *511 Prince Street*
Henry McKee House /Robert Smalls House
1834

This house is thought to have been built for Henry McKee in 1834. McKee sold the house to the DeTreville family about 1855. Robert Smalls was born a slave in 1839 in one of the cabins which stood in the rear of the lot. He progressed from slave to ship pilot to army captain, National Guard general, legislator, congressman, and finally Collector of the Port of Beaufort. With prize money from the sale of the ship Planter, which he captured from Confederate forces at Charleston and delivered to Federal forces at Beaufort, he bought this house at a tax sale in 1863. The DeTrevilles sued to regain title of the house after the war and pursued the case all the way to the U.S. Supreme Court, which held Small's title valid. This test case decided the validity of all the wartime tax titles in South Carolina. The property remained in the Smalls family until 1940. The McKees returned to Beaufort after the war, and Mrs. McKee, then quite old, wandered into the house one day thinking she was home. Robert Smalls installed her in her old room, and there waited on her as if she were still mistress of the house, until the day she died. Robert Smalls' remarkable life is chronicled in his biography, The Captain of the Planter by Dorothy Sterling. This house was designated a National Historic Landmark in 1975.

52. *502 Prince Street*
"Pretty Penny"
1885

George Edward Doane is thought to have built this small but pleasing house of simple Victorian architecture in 1885 of the choicest lumber from the lumber yard in which he worked. Each room has its own fireplace and wood closet. Before the house was begun, the extremely low lot was filled in with palmetto logs to increase the elevation.

53. *702 Hamilton Street*
Esther Foy Jenkins House
circa 1928

No building is shown on this site on the 1924 Sanborn Insurance Company Map. The lot on which this house was built was a present from South Carolina Senator Thomas Talbird to his youngest daughter, Christine, who had married Heyward Jenkins, an attorney. The cottage was built about 1928 for Jenkins' mother, Esther Foy Jenkins.

54. *201 Laurens Street*
Berners Barnwell Sams House (No. 2)
1852

Dr. Berners Barnwell Sams, a local planter and part owner of Datha (now known as Dataw) Island, is thought to have built this house in 1852. Facing an open area which is part of the property and long known as the "Front Green," the Sams house is a fine example of Classic Revival architecture. The dependency, which has been converted into apartments, is said to have contained a blacksmith shop, cook house with a great fireplace, a laundry, storeroom, and rooms for the household slaves. The house was used as Union Hospital #8 during the Civil War. It was bought by William Wilson at a U.S. Tax Commission sale and later served as the St. Helena Episcopal Church rectory, housing the Reverend A. P. Hay, the "poet of the Confederacy." Since 1895-96 this house has been owned by descendants of George Crofut. Of brown-toned plantation brick, four sturdy brick Doric pillars support a flat roof with a balustrade around the top and a two story verandah and give the house a handsome, massive look.

55. *1 Laurens Street*
Edgar Fripp House, "Tidalholm"
circa 1853

Edgar Fripp reportedly built this large Italianate style frame house to use as his summer home when the heat and mosquitoes made life at his plantation home on St. Helena Island intolerable. His brother, James Fripp, owned the house at the time of the Civil War. During the war, the house served as Union Hospital #7. Used as a guest house from the 1930s until 1974, "Tidalholm" brought to Beaufort as guests many artists, authors, professors, and statesmen. Set high off the ground in the center of an oak shaded lot, the house is almost encircled by the Beaufort River. Extensively altered after the "great hurricane" of 1893, an original tower and grouping of gabled roof elements no longer survives. Restored in 1974 as a private residence, it has kept its air of charm and gracious living. According to Fripp family legend, when James Fripp returned after the war he arrived just as the house was being sold for taxes by the U. S. Tax Commission. Unable to bid on the house, he stood with tears coursing down his cheeks. A Frenchman, who had been living in the area and who was sympathetic to the South, purchased the house. He is said to have walked over to the former owner, presented him with the deed, kissed him upon both cheeks, and left, returning to France before Mr. Fripp had a chance to repay him.

56. *207 Hancock Street*

Elizabeth Hext House, "Rivervew"
circa 1780

This house has long been considered one of the oldest houses in Beaufort. Traditionally referred to as the Elizabeth Hext House, its date of construction has been cited anywhere from 1700 to 1780, but surviving architectural evidence is most consistent with the later date. Elizabeth Hext, the only child of Francis Hext, Jr. and Elizabeth Stanyarne was born in 1746. At the age of fifteen she married William Sams of Wadmalaw Island, grandson of "Tuscarora Jack" Barnwell. In 1783, Sams bought Datha Island, near Beaufort, where the couple lived and raised a large family. When Elizabeth Hext Sams died in 1813, she was buried beside her husband on Datha Island. By 1862, the house was owned by Caroline E. Fripp, the daughter of Lewis Reeve Sams, who married James Fripp. The property was sold at the Direct Tax Sale in February 1863 to Samuel Cohen. The original house consisted of upper and lower piazzas, a narrow central hall flanked by two rooms on the main floor, and a rear hall and staircase which led to two bedrooms upstairs. A quality of intimacy pervades the house due to its relatively small scale when compared to the houses of the later antebellum period. The two front rooms have wainscot paneling around three walls with floor-to-ceiling paneling on the exterior fireplace walls. Interior walls are the thickness of only one plank, which indicates that the house is supported mainly by the exterior walls.

57. *804 Pinckney Street*
John Archibald Johnson House
circa 1850

Dr. John Johnson and his wife, Claudia Talbird, are thought to have built this three-story house in the 1850s. The house was still owned by Dr. Johnson at the opening of the Civil War and was used during the war as a part of Union Hospital #3. In 1973, a chimney collapsed in the house destroying a portion of its rear wall. Unable to repair the damage or to find a purchaser, its owner was forced to apply for a demolition permit in May 1974. After the permit was granted, the Historic Beaufort Foundation stepped in and purchased the property. It was resold to new owners who restored it. This sophisticated town residence was built in a period of high prosperity, and planned for formal living on a grand scale. A suite of rooms opens to the piazzas, allowing for sun in winter, shade and southerly breeze in summer. There are front and rear interior stair halls, fireplaces topped with wood or marble, and marble mantels in every room. The wide flooring, molding, doors, and paneled window frames are of local heart-pine.

58. *313 Hancock Street*

Talbird-Sams House
1786

This house is thought to have been built in 1786 by Henry Talbird. This date is not documented, however structural evidence including the conjectured original porch form, tabby basement and molding details strongly support a late-eighteenth century date. The house was later owned by Dr. Lewis Reeve Sams, Jr., who sold it to Thomas Talbird. The house was part of Union Hospital #3 in 1862. The interior has very fine wainscoting and dentil trim at the ceilings. The upper floor is one room deep and originally had a Palladian window at the stair landing.

59. *Corner of Hancock and Hamilton Streets*

Talbird House staircase
circa 1820

This site retains the ruins of a tabby house and outbuildings. The house has been lost almost entirely above ground except for main entrance steps. These comprise a single flight, fabricated of solid brick with marl or brownstone treads and an iron handrail. Probably built by Col. Thomas Talbird, stylistic evidence suggests a date of construction about 1795 to 1800. The house burned in The Great Bonfire of 1907.

60. *409 Hancock Street*
Chaplin House
circa 1843

It is not known for whom this house was built in 1843, but a balustrade holds a pearl amity button inset bearing that date. In 1860 John F. Chaplin purchased the house from John S. Fyler. This beautifully proportioned house is constructed with brick columns approximately eight feet apart resting on a tabby foundation supporting the main sills located at the second level. Wall studs are secured in the sills, both top and bottom, by mortise and tenon. The framework of mortised and doweled construction is principally heart-pine with random width flooring. During the Civil War the house was occupied by Union soldiers, some of whose names and regiments, written in chalk, can still be seen on the attic door. John F. Chaplin was able to recover the property in 1867 and his descendants still retained the property in 1999.

61. *708 East Street*
"The Tree House"
circa 1875; moved circa 1910

Tradition indicates that this house was
moved to this location by the Robert
Smalls family around 1910. The house
previously was situated on the property
known as Emmons farm at the corner of
Carteret and Boundary. In recent years,
the missing porches were replaced and a
small wing was added. See the description
of 511 Prince Street for more information
about Robert Smalls.

62. *508 Duke Street*
circa 1900

Cartographic sources suggest this
structure was an outbuilding associated
with 715 New Street. If so, it was present
on this site by 1912. According family
tradition, the house was built by Robert
Smalls as one of several rental units in the
late 1800s.

63. *715 New Street*
circa 1870

Originally two rooms over two, this house
has had a wing added to its rear elevation.
The house is thought to have been owned
by both Robert Smalls and his son-in-law
Samuel Bampfield. The original two-tier
full facade front porch has been replaced
by a simple stoop

64. *712 New Street*
Chaplin House
circa 1791

The architectural style of the house and an incised inscription found on a staircase suggest that its first phase of construction took place in 1791. Benjamin Chaplin was most likely the builder. The house was owned by Martha S. Chaplin Baynard in 1861. When this house was sold by the U. S. Tax Commission in 1863, it was reportedly purchased by a newly freed African-American woman. Her family owned it continuously until the early 1930s. Chlotilde Martin, a local journalist, later owned the house. In the mid-1940s, she was an organizer of the Committee to Save the Lafayette Building (now known as the Verdier House, 801 Bay Street) and later, in 1967, a founding member of Historic Beaufort Foundation.

65. *800 Carteret Street*
Beaufort College Building
1852

The Beaufort College was chartered in 1795 and opened in 1804. The first permanent college building was built at the corner of Bay and Church Streets in 1809. After the yellow fever epidemic of 1817, the college was relocated to the corner of Newcastle and Craven Streets and remained there until 1852. Robert W. Barnwell, an 1815 alumnus of Beaufort College and later a U.S. Congressman (1828-1832) and U. S. Senator (1850), served as a trustee of the Beaufort College and was instrumental in having the present building constructed. Designed by John G. Barnwell and built in 1851-1852, the building originally contained two classrooms, two offices, and a library. The library was designed as a miniature of the South Caroliniana Library in Columbia and housed the classical collection of the Beaufort Library Society. The college closed in 1861 due to the Union occupation. It served as the headquarters of the Freedman's Bureau during Reconstruction and became the Beaufort Elementary School in 1909. In 1959, the site was acquired by the University of South Carolina for a branch campus.

66. *502 Washington Street*
Kinghorn House
circa 1913; moved 1981

The Kinghorn family built this house circa 1913 on a lot at 406 Carteret Street. It was later purchased by the Carteret Street Methodist Church and used as a parsonage. It was eventually converted for use as the Church's youth center, acquiring the name "The Mustard Seed" from the children. The house was moved in 1981 to its present location and restored as a single family residence.

67. 500 Washington Street

Trescot House
circa 1860; rebuilt 1876; moved 1975

William Henry Trescot, historian and diplomat, built this house on Barnwell Island Plantation shortly before the Civil War. Among his many diplomatic posts, Trescot served as Secretary of Legation at London in 1852 until 1854 and was appointed assistant Secretary of State by President Buchanan in 1860. An 1863 account by William Howard Russell, an English war correspondent, describes what was perhaps this house in its original setting: "The planter's house is quite new, and built by himself the principal material being wood, and most of the work being done by his own Negroes. Such work as window-sashes and panellings, however, was executed in Charleston. A pretty garden runs at the back, and from the windows there are wide stretches of cotton fields visible, and glimpses of the river can be seen." Colonel William Elliott dismantled the house in 1876, brought it by boat to Beaufort, and erected it at 1011 Bay Street. In 1975. The Historic Beaufort Foundation was instrumental in saving the house and its subsequent relocation and restoration by Mr. & Mrs. Jack Treanor.

68. *411 Bayard Street*
The Rev. Thomas E. Ledbetter House
circa 1840

This excellent Beaufort-style house has an unusually fine setting with a magnificent view of the river from the two-story verandah which extends halfway along two sides of the house. Local tradition attributes construction of this house to the Rev. Thomas E. Ledbetter, a Methodist missionary who arrived in Beaufort about 1834. Ledbetter acquired the property circa 1840 from Thomas Talbird, who had purchased it from William G. Baynard in 1838. On a piece of hand-split lath found in the building in recent years was written "T. E. Ledbetter and Martin Eaddy missionaries at Beaufort and neighboring islands 1840 February." Another note found behind a mantelpiece in the living room read: "G. A. Laurence 1840." Ledbetter sold the property to the Rev. Stephen Elliott, who in turn sold in on 1 March 1858 to Louis M. DeSaussure, a physician. DeSaussure retained ownership until 1862, when it was taken by the U.S. Direct Tax Commission. It was sold in 1864 to William Lewis and Lorenzo Barrows, who in turn sold it to Charles H. Campbell in 1865. The Campbells retained the property until 1871, when it was sold to George Holmes. Holmes' son-in-law Neils Christensen acquired the property in 1881 and his family retained ownership until the 1960s. Christensen had served in the Union Army and was appointed as the first Superintendent of the Beaufort U.S. National Cemetery.

69. *505 Wasington Street*
"Petit Point"
circa 1855

This house is said to have been built for a spinster daughter of the Chaplin family. If so, this would suggest a construction date of circa 1850-1855. The property was held as two parcels just before the Civil War, the northern parcel owned by McGrath and the southern parcel by Arnot. The Sanborn Insurance Map for 1912 shows the present house as a two-story main structure with a two-story south porch and a one-story accommodation to the north. Before its restoration this house was generally considered beyond repair. Now it is a prime example of the inherent charm of many of Beaufort's small house

70. *507 Wasington Street*
John Fripp Chaplin Sr. House; "Chaplin Court"
circa 1815

Local tradition has held that this house was originally built ca. 1815 for John Fripp Chaplin Sr., a local planter with land holdings in both St. Helena and Prince William parishes. Chaplin is listed as owning the property in 1862, just prior to its sale by the U.S. Direct Tax Commission. Chaplin was unable to reclaim his property and it was sold instead to Israel Cohen. Cohen was an African-American who served in the First South Carolina Volunteers, the Union's first authorized Black unit. Dr. Joshua A. Whitman purchased the house from Cohen in 1869 and resided there until his death in 1905. His daughter Grace Whitman Bristol, wife of Beaufort jeweler and mayor William Read Bristol, inherited the property. In 1931, Sea Islands Real Estate, Inc., with Kate Gleason and her sister Eleanor as principals, purchased the property. Their remodeling of the Chaplin House into Chaplin Court, a five-unit apartment house, resulted in the enclosure of former porches and other substantial alterations. The wrought metal sign reerected over the entrance path dates from this period. These changes were reversed during a restoration in 1993.

Downtown
Neighborhood

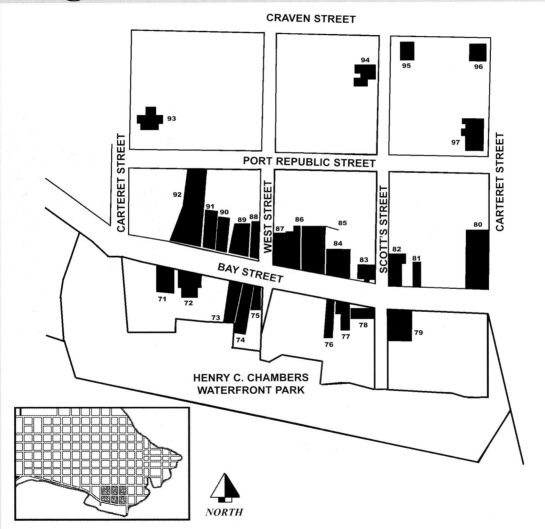

CRAVEN STREET

PORT REPUBLIC STREET

BAY STREET

HENRY C. CHAMBERS
WATERFRONT PARK

CARTERET STREET

WEST STREET

SCOTT'S STREET

CARTERET STREET

NORTH

Beaufort's historic commercial area has had a rich and varied history. As it developed in the early 1800s, merchants built fine dwellings with separate store buildings nearby. Dockyards, piers, and steamboat landings extend along the waterfront. Eventually, the dwellings were converted or replaced by commercial buildings and the street pattern evolved into the dense retail sector we see today. Vestiges of the earlier period survive in such buildings as the Verdier and Saltus Houses, yet most of the surviving buildings date from the late 1800s through the mid-20th century.

71. *928 Bay Street*
Beaufort Bank
circa 1916, remodeled 1947, 1988

The Beaufort Bank Company purchased this site in 1914 and the present Beaux Arts style building was completed by 1916. The bank closed in 1926 and the building was used intermittently as offices until 1947. In that year, two local businessmen acquired the building and converted it into a motion picture theater. Extensive alterations were made, including the removal of the front columns and the addition of an auditorium to the rear. The Breeze Theatre operated until the 1980s. The building was again remodeled in 1988 and the front columns were restored. The original columns had been used to construct a seawall after their removal in 1947. Their capitals were in use as driveway markers.

72. *920 Bay Street*
Abraham Cockcroft House
circa 1857

Abraham Cockroft is thought to have built this building as a residence circa 1857. The Greek Revival style facade of the house faces the Beaufort River. In the late 1800s and early 1900s, the building served as Beaufort's Customs House and Robert Smalls maintained an office there from 1899 through 1912. The building was purchased by William Joseph Thomas in 1932 and converted for use as retail and office space.

73. *910 Bay Street*
Luther's Pharmacy
1884

This two-story frame commercial building was constructed in 1884, as evidenced by the 1884 Sanborn Company insurance map of Beaufort which shows it under construction. Luther's Pharmacy occupied the building in the early twentieth-century.

74. *904 Bay Street*
circa 1875

This two-story frame commercial building was probably built circa1875 as part of the Wallace and Danner Dry Goods Store.

75. *902 Bay Street*
circa 1874 ca.

Apparently built circa 1874, the 1899 Sanborn map indicates the building housed a jewelry store. The two-story frame building is similar in character to both 902 and 904 Bay Street.

Historic Beaufort

812 Bay Street circa 1863   *812 Bay Street circa 1895*

76. *812 Bay Street*
Captain Francis Saltus Store
1796

Perhaps no site in Beaufort illustrates the frustration caused by the scarcity of pre-Civil War records more than this one. Local folklore has long held that John Cross built a tavern here in the early 1700s. Petitions to the South Carolina Legislature show this tabby structure was in fact erected by Captain Francis Saltus circa 1796 as a ship's store. There is no evidence that the present building functioned as a tavern until this century and the historical record indicates that no building was located here prior to this one. James I. Barnwell mortgaged this "tabby store and other outbuildings" to Charles H. Barnwell in 1866. Shown as a dry goods store in 1884, the property was acquired by the Chakides family in 1935 and has been used as a restaurant and tavern since that time. As originally constructed, the building was two stories tall with a gable roof oriented perpendicular to Bay Street. The connecting structure spanning the alley between this building and the adjacent building at 808 Bay Street to the east was not shown in a Civil War era photo of the site. It does appear on the 1884 Sanborn map. A late-nineteenth century photograph of the buildings show an elaborate Victorian paint scheme that highlighted the architectural features of the building and included faux painting over the stucco of this building to make it appear as stone.

Present Day: *808 Bay Street*   *812 Bay Street*

77. *808 Bay Street*
circa 1890

This two story frame commercial building is shown on the 1884 Sanborn map of Beaufort as a drug store. The overhead connector between the building and 812 Bay Street is also indicated on the map, although the upper level porch is not shown as extending across the connector until the 1889 Sanborn map.

Captain Francis Saltus House circa 1865

78. *802 Bay Street*
Captain Francis Saltus House
circa 1796

This historically and architecturally significant three-story tabby house was built by Captain Francis Saltus in 1796. Saltus was a merchant with commercial connections in New York, Charleston, and the West Indies. There is strong archaeological evidence suggesting that Saltus had a boatyard behind the house where five gunboats were built for the U. S. Navy in 1808. A photograph taken during the Civil War shows the building largely as it was constructed, except that the eastern portion of the building had already been converted for commercial use by that time. Following the war, the property was bought at auction by D.C. Wilson. By the turn of the century, the entire first floor was converted into retail space. In the 1950s, the building was converted for use as a Belks Department Store. The entire first floor front and rear walls were removed at that time and a new addition constructed to the rear. Despite these alterations, the house is of particular significance as one of the tallest known surviving tabby structures. It is also known to be one of the earliest structures built on the south side of Bay Street which was left open to the Beaufort River down to the end of the 18th century.

79. *720 Bay Street*

Charles E. Danner and Co.
circa 1910

This one-story brick commercial block was constructed after the great fire of 1907 and before 1912. The 1912 Sanborn map shows the entire property occupied by Chas. E. Danner and Co. Inc. wholesale grocers. The building was divided into two units before 1924, when it housed Beaufort Wholesale Groceries and The Beaufort Gazette.

80. *701 Bay Street*

circa 1907,
remodeled circa 1950

This two-story brick commercial building occupies the site of the McKee House which was destroyed in the fire of 1907. The south section of the present building was built shortly thereafter. Fordhams Hardware Store has operated in the building since 1947.

81. *715 Bay Street*

DeSaussure Store
circa 1760, remodeled 1908

Recent archaeological excavation indicates that this structure was originally a store associated with a raised three story tabby house (now destroyed) erected circa 1765 on the adjacent lot to the east and owned by Daniel DeSaussure before the American Revolution. During the Revolution, the structure was purchased by the loyalist Quaker merchant Zephaniah Kingsley whose son and namesake later founded Kingsley Plantation in in Northwest Florida. After being damaged in the 1907 fire, the gable ends of the original building were removed, and a new timber framed upper story added. The building was used by the Sam Levin family from 1880 to 1926. The Levins operated a dry goods store and lived upstairs. In 1932, Mrs. Alex Levin remodeled the building for use as the Ideal Beauty Shop.

82. *723 Bay Street*

circa 1885

This building was constructed circa 1885. The 1884 Sanborn map shows two earlier buildings on the site with a notation that they were to be taken down. The present building is shown on the 1899 map as a grocery store. Newspaper accounts indicate that the building was damaged by the 1907 fire. By 1912, the building housed a hardware store and it remained in that use until recent years.

83. *801 Bay Street*

John Mark Verdier House
circa 1801

This prominent Federal-style mansion was built circa 1801 by John Mark Verdier I (1759-1827), a local merchant and planter, on land which before the American Revolution had belonged to another merchant, Francis Stuart. Rising to great stature and wealth before the Revolution trading in indigo, Verdier's fortune diminished as markets for indigo disappeared with the war. His financial troubles were made worse by heavy speculation in forfeited lands. After a short stay in a Charleston debtors' prison, Verdier returned to Beaufort and caught its next wave of prosperity: sea island cotton. Verdier was able to eclipse his earlier success, reestablishing his mercantile interests, acquiring extensive plantation holdings, and owning, by 1810, 216 slaves. Unfortunately his fortunes were short lived and by the 1820s Verdier had moved to Charleston. The inventory of his estate taken after his death show few possessions and give indication of his reduced circumstances and his gradual transfer of assets to his children in the later years of his life. The property is thought to have passed to his son John Mark Verdier II and his wife Caroline McKee. While no evidence of their acquisition has been located, Caroline purchased the site from the Commissioners for Direct Tax in 1866, following John Mark II's death in 1857. The house remained in the family of Verdier's heirs into the twentieth century. It eventually ceased to be used as a single family residence, as apartments and businesses gradually took over its interiors. By 1942, the house had declined to such an extent that it was condemned. With rumors of the imminent replacement of the house by a gas station, a group of farsighted Beaufort citizens rallied to the defense of the house. Beaufort's first major community historic preservation project succeeded when the Committee to Save the Lafayette Building acquired the house in 1946. The Committee subsequently rehabilitated the property for use as rental space and in 1967 gave the property to its successor organization, the Historic Beaufort Foundation. The Foundation restored the house in 1976 and now operates it as a headquarters and an interpretive center illustrating the architectural heritage of the city of Beaufort.

84. *807 Bay Street*
circa 1885

The 1884 Sanborn map does not show this building, but it is shown on the 1899 map. At that time, it was divided into three separate retail units, including a clothing store, a dry goods store, and a general store. The building is located on the site of a former eighteenth-century tabby dwelling, often referred to as the Fripp House. The remnants of a tabby wall at the rear of the property are thought to have been related to that house.

85. *807 Bay Street (rear)*
circa 1800

This tabby wall is thought to be a remnant of the outbuilding complex for an eighteenth-century tabby house that was formerly located on the site. The 1884 Sanborn map shows a one-story concrete shed at this location. Sanborn maps of the period often referred to tabby buildings as concrete.

86. *815 - 819 Bay Street*
circa 1910

This two story, three-unit commercial building is first shown on the Sanborn map of 1912. Businesses operating in the building at that time included a bakery, a clothing store, and a furniture store. The 1905 Sanborn map shows the former G. M. Pollitzer Cotton Warehouse on the site as old and vacant.

87. *825 Bay Street*
Lipsitz Building
circa 1880

The 1884 Sanborn map of Beaufort shows this building with three commercial units, a millinery shop, a dry goods store, and a grocery and liquor store. Max and Bertha Lipsitz, Lithuanian immigrants, purchased the building circa 1902 and opened a general store.

88. *901 Bay Street*
circa 1890

Built circa 1890, this two story frame commercial building is first shown on the 1899 Sanborn map as a drug store. By 1912, it was shown as a dry goods store. The Bay Street facade is crowned by an elaborate cornice supported by paired decorative brackets.

89. *905-907 Bay Street*
Chisholm House
circa 1770

Despite extensive alterations, this house is historically significant as one of only four buildings built originally as residences along the three commercial blocks of Bay Street. Architectural evidence suggests it was built in the mid to late 1700s or early 1800s, making it perhaps the earliest of the four. It is shown on an 1861 engraving of federal troops marching down Bay Street during the initial occupation of Beaufort. The engraving and photographs taken during the war show the building with a less than full-facade one-story porch, interior or end chimneys with arched caps, and gable dormers. The house is shown on the 1905 Sanborn map as a "Bank & Dwelling." The house was occupied in 1909 by Dr. & Mrs. McPherson Gregory Elliott. Rosenthal's Dry Goods store occupied the first floor by the early 1930s.

915 Bay Street   *913 Bay Street*

90. *913 Bay Street*
circa 1920

This two story commercial building was not shown on the 1912 Sanborn map, but is indicated on the 1924 edition.

91. *915 Bay Street*
Schein Building
circa 1898

The Edwards Building, Bay Street facade

92. *917 Bay Street*
Edwards Building
1954

This building was built for the Edwards Department Store chain in 1954. Elliott Constantine, of Charleston, served as the principal architect with Beaufort architect Jules Levin, as an associate on the project.

The Edwards Building, Port Republic Street facade

93. *915 Port Republic Street*
Lucius Cuthbert House
circa 1820; remodeled circa 1875

Construction of this two-story frame house is attributed to Lucius Cuthbert in 1820. Built over a high brick foundation, the original house was one room deep with two cypress paneled rooms and other rooms with wainscoting and plaster walls. The Cuthberts, who owned the property just prior to the Civil War, moved to Aiken, South Carolina when Beaufort was occupied and never again lived here. During the occupation, the Federal Army used the house for a bakery. Acquired in 1875 or 1876 by F. W. Scheper, the house was changed by the addition of a second floor verandah, the cupola, the storm entrance, and the handsome fence which bears the Scheper name.

94. *308 Scott's Street*
The Beaufort Female Benevolent Society
circa 1895

The Beaufort Female Benevolent Society, an organization continuing today, was founded in 1814 to educate and provide for the relief of destitute children. This house was built by the Society in 1895 to provide income for the needy. It was occupied by the Circulating Library of the Clover Club from 1910 until the Carnegie Library on Craven Street was built in 1917. Subsequently, the house served as an infirmary and was shown as a dwelling on the 1924 Sanborn map.

95. *706 Craven Street*
Beaufort Municipal Meat Market
circa 1911

This building was constructed about 1911 as the Municipal Meat Market. The decision to build this building and its sister building at 702 Craven Street, was made while W. F. Sanders was serving as the Intendant (mayor) of Beaufort. Sanders was criticized for the high cost of the project, reportedly $11,000. The building was converted for use as a fire station by 1924.

96. *702 Craven Street*
Beaufort City Hall
circa 1911

One of two similar structures erected during or just before 1911 on the site of the former municipal market, this building originally housed a fire station. By 1924, the fire station was moved to 706 Craven Street and this building was converted for use as the Beaufort City Hall.

Historic Beaufort

97. *302 Carteret Street*
Post Office and Custom House, City Hall

Public notice that Beaufort was to receive a new post office appeared in the March 7, 1913 issue of the Beaufort Gazette. Congressman James F. Byrnes sent word to the city of plans to erect a $50,000 building once a suitable site was acquired. The present building was completed, according to its date-stone, in 1917 with James Witmore serving as supervising architect. It was converted for use as the Beaufort City Hall in recent years.

The Bluff Neighborhood

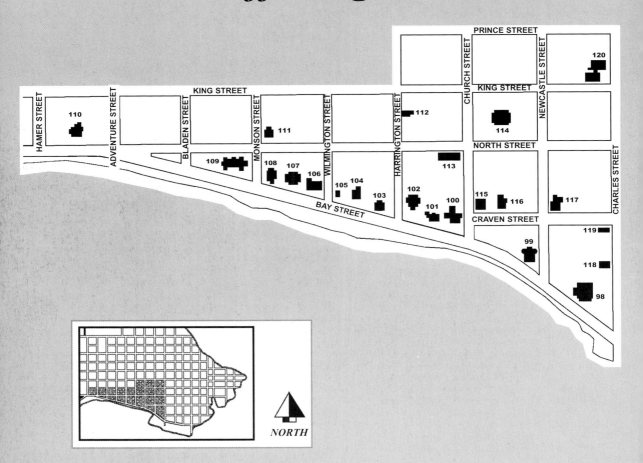

NORTH

The Character of the Bluff Neighborhood is dominated by its grand Bay Street promenade, along which gracious mansions overlook the bay from a high bluff. Spanish moss waves through ancient oak trees as the ever-present breeze comes up the Beaufort River. The neighborhood is also home to three of Beaufort's historic churches and the former county courthouse.

98. *1001 Bay Street*
George Parsons Elliott House
circa 1844

When George Parsons Elliott built this house about 1840, it had no upper verandah and the four massive pillars rose to the roof unimpeded. The second story verandah was added in the late-nineteenth century. Among the many excellent features of the house are a fine fanlit doorway, attractive iron railings, and good interior details including marble mantels, gilded cornices and moldings. Dr. William Jenkins, who owned over 1500 slaves and was one of the richest men in Beaufort, acquired the house before the Civil War. It was later purchased by George Holmes at a Direct Tax Commission sale during the war. His wife, Julia Hazel Holmes, lived in the house until her death in the 1930s. The house subsequently became a house museum in 1969. It was later acquired by The Historic Beaufort Foundation, which resold it to new owners who adapted it for use as offices in 1994.

99. *1103 Bay Street*
Elliott House. "The Anchorage"
Pre-Revolutionary, remodeled circa 1910

While Elliott was strongly pro-Southern and in favor of slavery, he opposed Secession and resigned his seat in the Senate rather than vote for Nullification. He regarded Robert Barnwell Rhett, leader in the Secession movement, as "unscrupulous" and "malignant." His was one of the voices of restraint heard in the town. He remained a staunch Unionist until the war broke out, when, like Robert E. Lee, he returned loyal to his state. During the Union occupation of Beaufort the house was used as a hospital and designated the Mission House. It was greatly altered in the 1900s by a retired Naval officer, Admiral Beardsley. He spent $80,000 remodeling it, adding stucco to the exterior and ornately carved woodwork to the interior. Later, the house was used as a guest house for many years. Threatened by demolition in 1971, "The Anchorage" was saved by Historic Beaufort Foundation, which, with the aid of a small group of friends, purchased the property and later resold it to a sympathetic owner.

100. *1203 Bay Street*
John A. Cuthbert House
circa 1810

The circumstance of the construction of this house has been lost to two competing legends over the years. The first suggests that it was built near Wyers Pond, but after much sickness and several deaths, the family decided that the location was unhealthy and had the house sawed in half and moved to its present site. The other indicates that it was built as a Presbyterian Manse and was acquired and moved by the Cuthbert family. Neither legend has been substantiated, yet both have plausible elements.

The front portion of the house appears to have been built circa 1810 and it underwent significant remodeling in the late 1830s or early 1840s. In 1862, the property was left to Sarah B. Cuthbert by the will of her mother Mary B. Stuart. Stuart was the widow of John Alexander Cuthbert II, the second son of James Hazzard Cuthbert. Union General Rufus Saxton purchased the home by Certificate # 249 at the Direct Tax Auction 1865. The book <u>Marching With Sherman</u>, written by an aide of General W. T. Sherman, contains the following passage: "The General came to Beaufort and stayed one day at General Saxton's. The latter owns a large fine double house on Bay Street fronting the s. He bought it at one of the U. S. Tax Sales and I was told gave $1,000 for it." The property was sold to Saxton's friend and agent Duncan C. Wilson in 1882. Wilson had been responsible for the construction of hundreds of prefabricated houses and military buildings on Hilton Head Island during the Civil War. Wilson is thought to have added Victorian style elements to the house, including the gingerbread trim and expansions to the south porch.

101. *1207 Bay Street*
Robert Means House
circa 1800

As with many Beaufort houses, the construction and early history of this substantial dwelling is not well documented. Most often attributed to Robert Means (1774-1832), a prominent Beaufort merchant and planter, the property is also thought to have been owned by John Bull circa 1800. If the latter is true, it is possible Means acquired the site from Bull, as the house was in the hands of the Means family at time of a Direct Tax Sale in the 1860s. George Gage, an Ohio native and later chief engineer of the Port Royal Railroad, purchased the house in 1872. Gage was also a prominent Republican who lost out to Robert Smalls in the selection of a new Collector of Customs in 1889. The house remained in Gage's family until 1919, when it was sold to Major Edward Denby of Michigan. Denby was appointed Secretary of the Navy under President Warren G. Harding and was among the cabinet members accused in the Teapot Dome scandal of 1923.

102. *1211 Bay Street*
Thomas Fuller House. "Tabby Manse"
1786

Tabby Manse is considered one of the finest early houses in Beaufort. Its design is similar to the Elizabeth Barnwell Gough House, constructed in 1780 on Washington Street. The house contains eight perfectly proportioned rooms, including three completely paneled in heart-pine and cypress. It has excellent Adam-style mantels, a superbly crafted stairway, a fine Palladian window in the rear elevation and a paneled second-floor drawing room. The two-foot thick exterior walls are made of tabby. The house was built circa 1786 as the residence of Thomas Fuller. During the Civil War, the house was purchased at the Direct Tax sale of 1864 by the Rev. Mansfield French, a Methodist minister sponsored by the American Missionary Association of New York City. In the 1870s, Almira Morill Onthank converted the house into a guest house and it was operated for more than a century by Onthank and her descendants. Francis Griswold wrote his Civil War novel A Sea Island Lady while staying in the house. This novel gives a glimpse into the life of old Beaufort.

103. *1301 Bay Street*
Leverett House
Early 1800s, moved circa 1850

Local tradition has long held that this house was moved to Bay Street from St. Helena Island by Dr. Benjamin Rhett around 1850. Charles Edward Leverett purchased it for $1,800 in 1854. After the Civil War, the Reverend Leverett, the last rector of Old Sheldon Church, wrote from Columbia the following letter to General Saxton: "Sir, I am the owner of a home in Beaufort, the 5th from the west end of the Bay, and a plantation on the Main, one mile from Garden's Corner on the lower road to Pocotaligo, on the right hand side across and bordering Huspah Creek. From the latter place, I was ordered by the Confederate picketry. I have taken the oath required by the U.S. and now write to claim my property. Colonel Ely informed me that I was to address you and said there would not be the least difficulty in my recovering the home. I am an Episcopal clergyman and have been in the exercise of my dismal engagements throughout the war at this place. Will you inform me in regard to the above? You are aware that we cannot, on account of the climate, return to our places until after frost, and then I do not know in consequence of what I hear of the occupation of the Negroes, if it would be possible at that time. You will oblige me, General, by addressing a letter to me stating if I can have my two homes and land. I am, respectfully your Obt. Svt., Charles Edward Leverett." More fortunate than most fellow townsmen, he regained ownership of his home after it had been confiscated during the war, and it remained in his family until 1920. The exterior of the house was restored in recent years, at which time the interior was completely remodeled.

104. *1305 Bay Street*
circa 1910

General Stephen Bull, a contemporary of "Tuscarora Jack" Barnwell, built a one-story cottage on this lot because he feared that a two-story structure could not withstand the strong winds and storms of the area. The present house, built in the early 1930s on the foundations of the original, is surrounded by a fine well-preserved cast-iron fence reportedly made from Swedish ore.

105. *1307 Bay Street*

William Ritchie House
circa 1883

Sitting primly and at ease amid its more imposing antebellum neighbors is this sturdy Victorian house. It was built about 1883 by William Ritchie, a foot soldier from Connecticut who came to Beaufort with the Northern Army and decided to remain.

106. *400 Wilmington Street*
(Facing Bay Street)
John Joyner Smith House
circa 1811, circa 1850

This house is thought to have been built by John Joyner Smith circa 1813. Smith's ownership is confirmed by the Direct Tax claim of his heir, Elizabeth Barnwell, in the 1860s. The house was originally constructed in the Federal style, as evidenced by the elaborate front entrance. Some time later, possibly in the 1850s, the house was extensively remodeled in the Greek Revival style. The principal entrance was moved to Wilmington Street and the present interior plan and detailing were added. The former entrance was retained as a false entrance.

During the Civil War, General Stevens, the Federal Military Commander, occupied the house with his staff. His aide, William Thompson Lusk, wrote his mother, "we are now pleasantly living in Beaufort with all sorts of comforts at our disposal. The house occupied by General Stevens is the one belonging to Mr. Smith and is an extremely elegant one. The portrait of Bishop Elliott looks down benignly from the mantel while I write. Personally I wish the owners were back in their homes." The smaller house at the back of the property, with its hand-hewn beams, is believed to be the original barn or carriage house.

107. *1405 Bay Street*
Edward Barnwell House
1785

This frame house of excellent massing with fine chimneys and a well-proportioned portico, was built by Edward Barnwell, the father of sixteen children, the last of whom was nicknamed Sally Sixteen. Edward Barnwell was the great-grandson of "Tuscarora Jack" Barnwell, the Indian fighter. During the Civil War Federal officers used the house for their quarters. They flattened one of the chimneys and erected a large platform on the roof from which the signal officer could send messages to naval vessels anchored down river. The interior has two excellent paneled rooms with Adam-style mantels, good woodwork and a handsome Palladian window at the stair landing. In the 1950s, the original slender columns and two piazzas were removed and replaced by Doric columns which rise to the roof unimpeded.

108. *1411 Bay Street*
E. A. Scheper House
1893

E. A. Scheper built this house with an intricate lace and gingerbread exterior in the 1890s, when it was a show place of Beaufort. In 1938 the house was bought and almost completely rebuilt, transforming the exterior from Victorian to antebellum revival. The rooms were enlarged and the cabinet-makers were brought to Beaufort to make the beautifully carved mantel in the library and to cut and place the random-width flooring and paneling.

109. *1501 Bay Street*
Beaufort County Courthouse
1883 / 1936

The Beaufort County Courthouse is Beaufort's most notable example of the Art Deco architectural style. Originally constructed in 1883/4 in a Victorian style, it was extensively remodeled to its present form in 1936. The present structure is located on the site of the Federal period house known as Barnwell Castle, fragments of which survive below ground as tabby foundations. The cornerstone for the Beaufort County Courthouse, as it was originally known, was laid on November 29th, 1883, and construction was completed the following year. In 1935, funding to remodel the courthouse was received from the Public Works Administration. J. Whitney Cunningham served as the project architect and Boyle Road and Bridge Co. served as the general contractor. Work was completed shortly after Thanksgiving 1936. The building opened as Beaufort District Federal Court following extensive restoration during 1995-96.

110. *1705 Bay Street*
William Keyserling House
"The Teacherage"
1917

The William Keyserling House was constructed in 1917 for Beaufort businessman William Keyserling and his wife Mary. Designed by Savannah architect Morton Levy, the house and grounds contained a servant's quarters (now 1711 King Street), a two-car garage, and clay tennis courts. The house featured indoor plumbing, a central vacuum system, a patented "Combined Needle and Shower Bath" full brass body shower, an electric call box system, and ample closets. In 1943, the property was sold to the Beaufort Board of Education and was used as a boarding house for female teachers, known as "The Teacherage." Last used by the Board of Education as offices in the 1960s, the house suffered several fires and sat vacant for many years. It was restored for use as a bed and breakfast, opening in 1990 as TwoSuns Inn.

111. *1411 North Street*
Emil E. Lengnick House
circa 1900

This house, in Queen Anne vernacular style, was built by Emil E. Lengnick around 1900. Since that time there have been no substantial changes to the house. Set at an angle so that the Beaufort River breezes could be enjoyed, the house is of heart pine construction with imbricated shingle siding. The turret with its steeply pitched roof shows the Gothic influence on the eclectic Victorian period architecture.

112. *509 Harrington Street*
circa 1860

This home is an example of a Charleston-style house, where the entrance is gained from a side porch. Left vacant for some years, the house was purchased and restored in the 1970s.

113. *First Presbyterian Church*
1201 North Street
1929

The First Presbyterian Church was established on 12 May 1912 with two elders and twenty-six other charter members. The sanctuary was constructed in 1929 and has been expanded at least twice. An Education Building was added across the street in 1959. The present temple-in-antis facade was created in 1983 when the former facade was extended one bay to the east.

114. *501 Church Street*
St. Helena's Episcopal Church
1817, 1842

The original St. Helena's Episcopal Church was built in 1724 to serve the parish established in 1712. This first building was replaced in 1769. In 1817, the 1769 building was extended to the west. The extension was retained in 1842 when the remainder of the church was demolished to ground level. The present side walls were constructed at that time and the foundations of the 1769 church were used to support the interior galleries. The chancel was destroyed in a hurricane in the 1890s and subsequently rebuilt in its present form. The upper level of the tower was constructed in 1942 and was designed by Albert Simons of Charleston.

During the Civil War, Federal troops adapted the church for use as a hospital, uprooting slabs from the graveyard for use as operating tables. The present altar was built and donated by the sailors of the U.S.S. New Hampshire, which was stationed here after the Civil War.

The cemetery surrounding the church, now enclosed by a brick wall, is highly important to local history. One of the first persons to be buried in the churchyard was Colonel John Barnwell, better known as "Tuscarora Jack." After leading successful raids against the troublesome Tuscarora Indians, Barnwell died in 1724. His grave, along with others, lies beneath the church. Two British officers, killed in a skirmish near Port Royal during the Revolution, were buried by Captain John Barnwell ("Tuscarora Jack"). Barnwell sent his sergeant into the church for a prayer book, read the burial service, and then said, "We have shown the British we not only can best them in battle, but that we can also give them a Christian burial." Also buried here are two Confederate Generals. One, Lt. General Richard H. Anderson, a West Pointer who resigned to serve the Confederacy, was with the South Carolina Brigade and fought at Williamsburg, Virginia. The other, Brigadier General Stephen Elliott, was Captain of the Beaufort Volunteer Artillery and the Charleston Battalion. He was sent to Virginia, made a Brigadier General and was wounded while defending Petersburg. In the parish house grounds, north side, are the graves of persons who, because of death from dueling or suicide, were not allowed burial in hallowed ground.

St. Helena's Episcopal Church

115. *1113 Craven Street*
Milton Maxcy House. "Secession House."
circa 1813

An inscription on the basement wall reads: "In this house the first meeting of Secession was held in South Carolina." Local tradition suggested further that "after voting, the Beaufort County Delegation went directly to the boat landing and set off for Charleston to cast their ballots for secession." Unfortunately, documentary evidence suggests that neither story is accurate. In fact, the name "Secession House," long associated with the property is appropriate, for the house was owned and substantially remodeled by leading South Carolina secessionist Edmund Rhett. It is said that a tabby house stood here before the Revolution. Around 1800 Milton Maxcy came to Beaufort from

Massachusetts to open a school for boys and acquired the property. He removed the tabby second floor, and added the two wood frame upper stories. Edmund Rhett, the next owner, remodeled the house in a modified Greek Revival style. The house was used by the Union Army for the billeting of officers, as a hospital, and for the office of the Paymaster.

116. *1109 Craven Street*
William Fickling House
1820s

This two-story clapboard house with Adam-style interior was built by William Fickling who taught in a boys' school. It is now the Rectory of St. Helena's Episcopal Church. The grounds extend through to North Street and give a view across the lawn of the beautiful south gate of the church. The original house was only one room deep. Surviving architectural elements indicates the house was built in the 1820s, although local tradition suggests an earlier date. The rear portion, including a bay window on the east, was added after the Civil War. Photographs made by the Federal Government at that time show an ell, with chimneys at the rear. The earliest known record of the house is 1807, when Mrs. Fickling sold the property after her husband's death.

117. *1009 Craven Street*

Thomas Rhett House
circa 1820

Similar to "Secession House," this is an excellently proportioned house with two-story wrap-around piazzas and transom-lighted doorways. The fine interior is accented by an arch of carved palmetto fans over the central hall. Renovations revealed beautiful original mantels in the two principal front rooms. The builder of the house is unknown; however, Thomas Rhett, with his wife Caroline Barnwell, lived here prior to the Civil War. He was the oldest of seventeen Smith children who changed their name to Rhett in honor of their great-great grandfather, William Rhett, whose family name had died out.

118. *308 Charles Street*
"Woodbine Cottage"
Pre-Civil War

In 1862, this property was owned by D.W. Jenkins and it was associated with the George Parsons Elliot House at 1001 Bay Street. The house is thought to have either been built or substantially remodeled in 1867. The house has often been referred to as "Woodbine Cottage," although the source of that name has not been documented.

119. *314 Charles Street*

Sarah Gibbes Barnwell House
circa 1855

The historic ownership of this house has long been attributed to Sarah Gibbes Barnwell (1788-1866). Sarah was the youngest daughter of Gen. John Barnwell and she never married. Stylistic evidence suggests the house was constructed circa 1855. It was definitely present by the time of the Civil War, as it is shown in a photograph that survives from the period.

120. *600 Charles Street*
Baptist Church of Beaufort
1844

In 1795, Henry Holcombe of the Euhaw Baptist Church moved to Beaufort where a small building was built for worship, probably on the present site of the Baptist Church. The church grew and in 1804 the Baptist Church of Beaufort was constituted. The present church was built at a cost of $10,000 and was first used on 14 April 1844. Deacon Joseph Hazel, a local planter, supervised the construction and Richard Fuller was pastor. In 1857, the congregation included about 180 whites and more than 3,500 slaves, many of whom were served by missions on the islands. The building was designated Hospital #14 during the Civil War.

One of Beaufort's finest Greek Revival landmarks, the beautifully proportioned interior has galleries on three sides that are supported by fluted Doric columns. The cove ceiling has unusually fine plaster ornamentation. The church was damaged by Hurricane Gracie in 1959 and the present steeple was added in 1961. A major renovation of the building was completed in 1998.

Northwest Quadrant Neighborhood

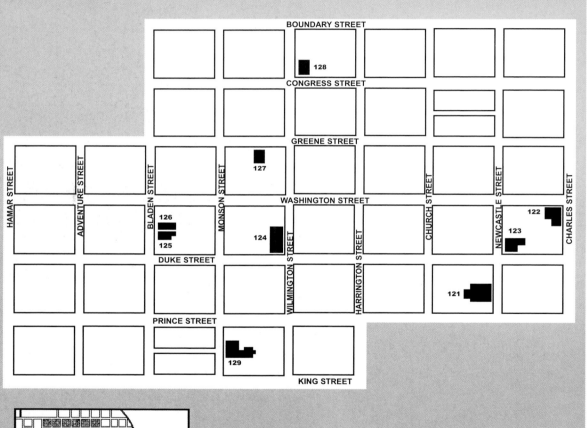

BOUNDARY STREET

128

CONGRESS STREET

GREENE STREET

127

HAMAR STREET

ADVENTURE STREET

BLADEN STREET

MONSON STREET

WASHINGTON STREET

CHURCH STREET

NEWCASTLE STREET

CHARLES STREET

122

123

126

125

124

WILMINGTON STREET

HARRINGTON STREET

121

DUKE STREET

PRINCE STREET

129

KING STREET

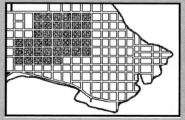

NORTH

Beaufort's Northwest Quadrant represents the city's largest traditionally African-American neighborhood. Developed after the Civil War, its modest folk style buildings reflect an important chapter in Beaufort's history. They are tangible reminders of the contributions made to the city by the many tradespeople, domestics, laborers, small business owners, and others who lived in the neighborhood.

121. *706 Newcastle St.*
Grand Army of the Republic
Meeting Hall
circa 1896

This building was constructed by African-American veterans as a chapter of the Grand Army of the Republic, a national Civil War veterans' organization. Beaufort is one of the rare southern cities to have had a substantial number of local African-American veterans of the war. Beginning with the fall of Beaufort in 1861, newly freed former slaves from the surrounding area joined the federal army. These veterans formed the David Hunter Post #9 of the G.A.R. after the war and acquired this property on 1 July 1896. It is reported to be the only surviving building in South Carolina associated with the group. Heavily damaged by fire in the early 1980s, it has since been restored.

122. *814 Charles Street*
Richard Washington, Jr. House
circa 1890

Richard Washington, Jr. purchased this property on 24 January 1877 from Ridley and Monday Williams. He constructed the present house sometime thereafter. Heavily damaged by fire in recent years, the house was restored as a project of Historic Beaufort Foundation's Revolving Fund.

123. *1013 Duke St.*
circa 1830

Thought to be the earliest house in Beaufort's Northwest Quadrant neighborhood, construction features on the interior suggest this house was built in the first third of the 1800s. It is shown on the map the Direct Tax Commission prepared during the Civil War under the ownership of Joseph W. Patterson.

124. *1401 Duke Street*
circa 1900

Corner stores were once a common element of Beaufort's historic district. This small market is one of the few to have survived. Construction details suggest it was constructed about 1900.

125. *809 Bladen Street*
circa 1895

Clara Forbes sold this "lot of land" to J.L. Johnson and Emma Stiles on 21 August 1893. The 1900 census lists Josiah Grant, an African-American ship's carpenter, living at the site, then known as 510 Bladen Street. A property transfer in 1906 records Lizzie Watson, Annie Stiles, and Grant as the heirs of Emma Stiles selling their 1/2 interest in the property "with improvements thereon" to N. Christensen. This house and its twin exhibit more elaborate architectural details than most of the other houses in this neighborhood.

126. *807 Bladen Street*
Robert Proctor House
circa 1895

Robert Proctor, an African-American carpenter, is listed in the 1900 census living at this address. Proctor was born in South Carolina in November 1858 and married his wife Annie about 1883. Stylistic evidence and documented sources for the twin house at 809 Bladen Street suggest that this house was built circa 1895.

127. *1408 Greene Street*
circa 1880

As the economic condition of former African-American slaves began to improve in Beaufort, so did the quality of the houses they built. 1408 Green Street is representative of the evolution of the Freedman's Cottage folk house type (see 1313 Congress Street) into a hall-and-parlor style.

128. *1313 Congress Street*
circa 1870

1313 Congress Street is similar to other simple folk houses built in coastal South Carolina by newly freed African-American slaves in the years immediately following the Civil War. Often referred to as "Freedman's Cottages," these houses were small one-story buildings with lateral gable roofs. Typically three bays wide and one bay deep, with a central entrance, these houses were plain in detail. 1313 Congress Street is the only example of this folk tradition remaining in the Beaufort Historic District.

129. *1409 King St.*
Beaufort County Jail
1938

The Beaufort County Jail is a well developed example of Art Deco/Moderne style of architecture in Beaufort. Constructed in 1938 on the site of an earlier jail, the building was designed by Beaufort architect Jules D. Levin. The large addition to the west was constructed in 1961.

The
Old Commons
Neighborhood

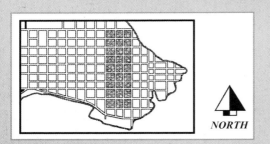

NORTH

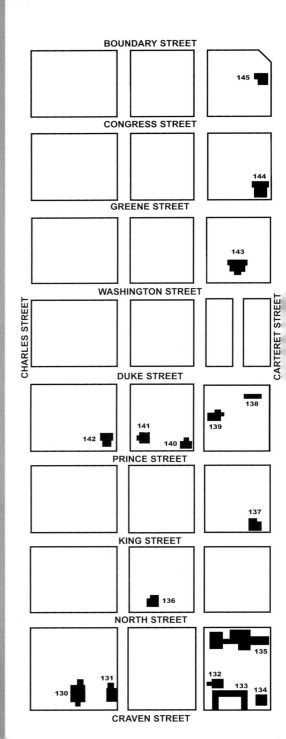

Mansions and cottages sit side by side in the Old Commons, Beaufort's most architecturally eclectic neighborhood. Churches and public buildings complete the assemblage of historic buildings that date from the beginning of the 1780s through the early-twentieth century.

130. *911 Craven Street*
Tabernacle Baptist Church
1840; circa 1893

The Tabernacle, a meeting house and lecture room, was built by Beaufort Baptist Church in the 1840s perhaps on site of a praise house built before 1832. On 1 September 1863, Tabernacle Baptist Church was organized by the Rev. Soloman Peck of Boston, Massachusetts, with much of its 500 member African-American congregation coming from the Beaufort Baptist Church. The new congregation acquired this building and continues to use it for worship. Damaged in the hurricane of 1893, it was rebuilt and rededicated. The cemetery contains graves of the Bythewood family, the earliest of which is dated 1817, suggesting an early-nineteenth century burial ground occupies the site.

A memorial to Robert Smalls is also located in the cemetery, where Smalls is buried. Robert Smalls (1839-1915) was born into slavery. In 1862, while working as part of the slave crew of the Confederate steamer "The Planter," Smalls managed to capture the ship and turn it over to Union forces. After the war, his distinguished career of public service included election to the South Carolina House of Representatives (1868-1870) and Senate (1870-1875), as well as five terms in the U. S. House of Representatives (1875-1879, 1882-1887). Smalls also served as a major general in the state militia and later served as Port Collector for Beaufort.

131. *901 Craven Street*

W. J. Jenkins House
circa 1845

Construction of this house is attributed to W. J. Jenkins about 1845. Although the present two-story portico is thought to have replaced an earlier verandah, this house is still a good example of the well-designed, finely proportioned Beaufort house. Four of the five fanlights are the originals, delicately cut glass in a Venetian pattern. During the Civil War the house was occupied by Union troops and afterward it became a hotel or boarding house known as the Saxton House.

132. *403 Scott's Street*

Congregation Beth Israel
1907

This meeting house for Beaufort's Jewish community was built in 1907. This property was sold by Nora Comerford to the Beth Israel congregation in 1905. An article in the 20 June 1907 <u>Beaufort Gazette</u> indicates that: "A lot had already been bought just back of the Arsenal, and considerable brick and other materials is now on the spot." The synagogue is first shown complete in its original form by the Sanborn Insurance Company map of 1912.

133. *713 Craven Street*
Beaufort Arsenal
1795; 1852

Construction of the Beaufort Arsenal was begun in 1795 and completed by 1799. The authorization by the state legislature in 1795 stated: "And be it further enacted, that General Barnwell, Thomas Grayson, and Ralph Elliott, be, and they are hereby appointed commissioners, and by virtue of this act, are fully authorized and empowered to purchase a lot or piece of land, and to erect and build thereon, at the old courthouse in the town of Beaufort, a magazine capable of containing a hundred thousand weight of gun powder and a thousand stand of arms, to enclose the same with a substantial brick wall...." Construction was entrusted to Col. Thomas Talbird. The building had deteriorated substantially by 1852, when the Beaufort Volunteer Artillery Company rebuilt the complex "on the foundation of the old Arsenal a building capable of accommodating a garrison of 250 men and a battery of six guns." The Beaufort Volunteer Artillery was organized in April, 1775 and is the fifth oldest military unit in the United States. For years it was housed in or connected with the Beaufort Arsenal. The building was enlarged and renovated in a 1934 WPA project. The Beaufort Museum occupied one of the wings and the National Guard occupied the main building. The city-owned museum now occupies the entire site. A portion of the original tabby structure survives incorporated into the later buildings.

134. *701 Craven Street*

Carnegie Library
1917

A plaque on the building's wall reads: "The Beaufort Township Library was built on property given to the Clover Club by the City, with the aid of Carnegie funds procured through the efforts of Senator Neils Christensen." The dedication stone records names of J. H. Sams, architect; J. H. Moore, contractor; and B.A.Cooper, Grand Master. The Clover Club is a volunteer organization that operated a circulating library at 308 Scott's Street prior to completion of this building in 1917. The club donated 2,000 books to the new facility. The building was converted for use as Beaufort's City Hall in 1963. A note added to the 1979 historic sites survey form for this property stated: "building was designed by James Hagood Sams – originally it had barrel (Roman) tile roof and ocular dormers – also – building was painted in the 1960s – original was red brick with gray mortar." The roof and dormers were reconstructed in 1999.

135. *408 Carteret Street*

Carteret Street Methodist Church

Beaufort's ties to Methodism began in 1737, when John Wesley, founder of the denomination, visited Beaufort while serving in Savannah as a priest of the Church of England. The community was first served by Methodist missionaries in 1833. By the Civil War, the local Methodist congregation erected a church on the corner of Prince and Church Streets (see Wesley United Methodist Church, site #141). During the war, that church became the property of the Methodist Episcopal Church North and began to serve an African-American congregation. In 1882, a frame church was built on the Carteret Street site. The growing congregation began planning for the present building by 1920 and work was begun on May 30, 1922.

136. *807 North Street*
circa 1835

This is a distinctive example of a one-and-one-half story dwelling with a rear "T" wing. Construction details suggest the house was built in the first half of the 1800s. The property was owned by "McGrath" in 1862 according to the U. S. Direct Tax Commission's map. Local tradition has often referred to this as the "Birthing House," because it was later the home of an African-American mid-wife.

137. *602 Carteret Street*
Berean Presbyterian Church
circa 1900

This building is indicated in its present configuration on the 1905 Sanborn Insurance map of Beaufort and was used as an African-American Presbyterian church until at least 1924. The building was purchased from the synod and became the library for the county's African-American residents from 1932 to 1965. Sold to Beaufort County Council in 1966, the building later became the Art Department of the University of South Carolina at Beaufort. A major renovation of the structure was conducted in 1993.

138. *710 Carteret Street*
Saint Peter the Apostle Roman Catholic Church
1846

Michael O'Conner, a devout Catholic from Ireland, arrived in Beaufort in 1822. Finding no church here, he made arrangements to have Mass said in his residence by Father Edward Quigley, who made regular visits to Beaufort. Michael O'Conner, then owner of the Bay Street Hotel, later donated property for this church. St. Peter the Apostle's Church was dedicated in November 1846 by Bishop Ignatius Reynolds. Father Jeremiah J. O'Connell was named the parish priest. The building was remodeled in 1946.

139. *711 Prince Street*
Daniel Hingston Bythewood House
circa 1792

Daniel Hingston Bythewood, a British merchant and sea captain, is thought to have built this clapboard house for his wife, Elizabeth Taylor, who had persuaded him to give up his prosperous voyaging and become a Baptist missionary. Both he and his wife are buried in the Baptist churchyard. Built upon a high tabby foundation and braced by sturdy chimneys, the house looks out over a long sweep of lawn. The outstanding paneled interior includes hand-carved mantels and over-mantels, chair rails and wainscoting. Original wide pine flooring still exists in all rooms.

140. *801 Prince Street*

Miles Brewton Sams House
circa 1800

Local tradition relates that the builder of this house was Miles Brewton Sams. Architectural evidence suggests a construction date of circa 1800. The Sams family is cited as owner of the property on the 1862 Direct Tax Commission map of the city.

141. *701 West Street*
Wesley United Methodist Church
circa 1849

This church was constructed circa 1849 by Beaufort's Methodist congregation. During the Civil War, the property was acquired by the Methodist Episcopal Church North and the church was subsequently used by an African-American congregation which continues there.

142. *901 Prince Street*
Frederick Fraser House
circa 1803

Construction of this house has traditionally been attributed to Frederick Grimke Fraser circa 1803. According to his own testimony Fraser did not come into possession of this property until August 10, 1827. It is possible construction commenced soon thereafter. However, the style of doorcase and other details do suggest a date closer to 1800. The grandson of John Fraser, a Scottish immigrant who settled on plantations in Pocataligo and Coosawhatchie in 1700, Fraser died on February 7, 1852 and left the house to his wife Isobel Fraser and their children. The house is constructed of brick, eighteen inches thick and covered with stucco scored to simulate masonry blocks. Double stairs over a wide arch lead to a piazza where six slender fluted columns rise to meet those of a second-floor verandah. A Palladian doorway opens onto the upper verandah, and a window of the same style lights the stair landing.

143. *705 Washington Street*
Elizabeth Barnwell Gough House
circa 1780

The "Old Barnwell House" is one of a small group of Beaufort buildings based in their appearance on the Miles Brewton House in Charleston (circa 1765) and at a distant remove, the Palladian villas of the Venetian mainland. The "T" shaped house is constituted of tabby and illustrates aspects of the Adam and emerging Federal Styles. Thanks to the generosity of Mr. & Mrs. H. L. Pratt, III, paneling removed from the lower southeast parlor in the 1930s and later installed in a house in California, was returned as a gift to Historic Beaufort Foundation. The paneling was subsequently restored to the house by its then owners Colin and Jane Bruce Brooker.

Elizabeth Barnwell (1753-1817) was the granddaughter of "Tuscarora" Jack Barnwell. She married Richard Gough (1750-1796) of James Island in London in 1772. After a bitter quarrel, Richard and Elizabeth separated. Following the death of Elizabeth's father, Col. Nathaniel Barnwell, in 1775, this house was built for Elizabeth Barnwell Gough with money left for her benefit.

144. *701 Greene Street*

DeTreville House, "The Mission"
circa 1785

Believed to have been built by the Reverend James Graham who married Sarah Jane Givens of Beaufort, this frame house with tabby foundations has two fine exterior end-wall chimneys and other exterior detailing. Interior details include mantels, wainscoting, a mahogany staircase, and an original ceiling medallion in the drawing room. Graham was born in Scotland and served as the third pastor of the Baptist Church of Beaufort. In the mid-nineteenth century the Misses Fanny and Julia Baker lived in this house, which became known as the Baker house. Miss Julia was the author of the poem "Mizpah-God Watch Between Me and Thee," which was very popular during her day. The 1862 Direct Tax map indicates J.T. Baker as the owner of the property before the occupation of Beaufort by Union troops. The Misses Baker fled at the beginning of the Civil War. During Reconstruction, the house became known as "The Mission" and was occupied by Mrs. Rachel C. Mather and the Baptist missionaries who built Mather School for the "furtherance of Negro education" and who were active in the Freedmen's Aid Society.

145. *1106 Carteret Street*

John Conant House, The Bellamy Inn
circa 1880

This post-bellum house with its spectacular view of the river is a fitting introduction to the Historic District. Built of clapboard and distinguished by a mansard roof, the house is two-and-one-half stories tall. A double porch faces south. Dormer windows face north, south, east and west. Before the occupation of Beaufort by Union Troops in 1862, this property was owned by Margaret G. Milne, who also owned a plantation on Port Royal Island called Springfield, or Spring Hill, containing 400 acres. After the war, the site was purchased by John Conant of Bangor, Maine, who had served as a captain in the 8th Regiment of Maine. He tore down a small building on the site that had been used as a barracks during the war and built this house. His wife Elvira and his only daughter, Lucy, moved to Beaufort to make their home and Conant opened an ice house. Several times each year vessels came down from Maine bringing huge cakes of ice packed in sawdust. In December 1925, Mrs. P. E. Bellamy converted the house into a nine-room tourist inn and it operated in this capacity until the mid-1950s. Facing demolition in recent years, the house was purchased and completely rehabilitated. It has since served as an antique shop and offices. In 1997, the property was acquired by the Beaufort Chamber of Commerce for use as offices and a visitors' center.

Index

Sites listed by name

P

R

S

T

V

W

Sites listed by Address

Bay Street

Baynard Street

Bladen Street

Carteret Street

Pinckney Street

Port Republic Street

Prince Street

Scott's Street

Short Street

Washington Street

West Street

Wilmington Street